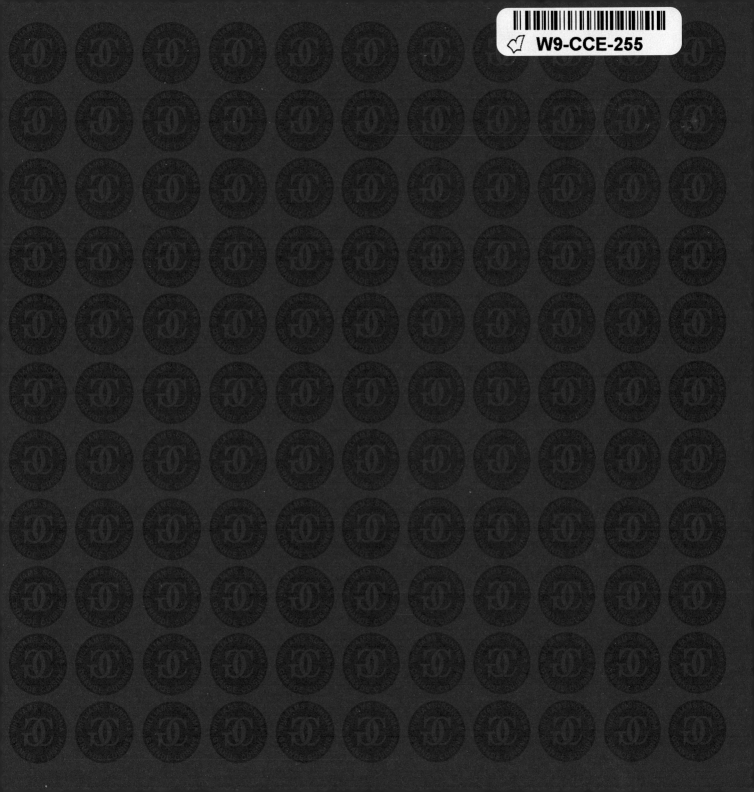

TIME-LIFE BOOKS
Time-Life Books is a division of Time Life Inc.
Time-Life is a trademark of Time Warner Inc. U.S.A.

Time-Life Custom Publishing
Vice President and Publisher: Terry Newell
Director of New Product Development: Regina Hall
Managing Editor: Donia Ann Steele
Director of Sales: Neil Levin
Director of Financial Operations: J. Brian Birky

WILLIAMS-SONOMA
Founder/Vice-Chairman: Chuck Williams

WELDON OWEN INC.
President: John Owen
Vice President and Publisher: Wendely Harvey
Vice President and CFO: Richard VanOosterhout
Associate Publisher: Laurie Wertz
Consulting Editor: Norman Kolpas
Copy Editor: Sharon Silva
Designer: Angela Williams
Production Director: Stephanie Sherman
Production Coordinator: Tarji Mickelson
Production Editor: Janique Gascoigne
Co-Editions Director: Derek Barton
Food Photographer: Allan Rosenberg
Additional Food Photography: Allen V. Lott
Primary Food Stylist: Heidi Gintner
Primary Prop Stylist: Sandra Griswold
Assistant Food Stylists: Nette Scott, Elizabeth C. Davis,
    Jeffrey Lord
Assistant Prop Stylist: Elizabeth C. Davis
Glossary Illustrations: Alice Harth

The Williams-Sonoma Kitchen Library
conceived and produced by Weldon Owen Inc.
814 Montgomery St., San Francisco, CA 94133

In collaboration with Williams-Sonoma
3250 Van Ness Ave., San Francisco, CA 94109

Production by Mandarin Offset, Hong Kong
Printed in China

A Note on Weights and Measures:
All recipes include customary U.S. and metric
measurements. Metric conversions are based on
a standard developed for these books and have
been rounded off. Actual weights may vary.

A Weldon Owen Production

Copyright © 1996 Weldon Owen Inc.
Reprinted in 1996

Library of Congress
Cataloging-in-Publication Data:

Holiday entertaining / general editor, Chuck Williams :
    photography, Allan Rosenberg.
        p.   cm. — (Williams-Sonoma kitchen library)
    Includes index.
    ISBN 0-7835-0317-2
    1. Holiday cookery.   2. Entertaining.   3. Menus.
    I. Williams, Chuck.   II. Series.
TX739.H6523   1996
642'.4—dc20   95-47662
                                              CIP

Contents

INTRODUCTION

It is sometimes said that good hosts and hostesses have an almost magical ability to make any meal seem like a holiday.

I think that such magic is actually found in a few simple guidelines anyone can follow when throwing a party: advance planning, thoughtful recipe selection, careful shopping and the preparation of some dishes well ahead of time. With such essentials under control, you are free to apply your imagination to other party details; and, better still, you're fresh enough to enjoy the event yourself.

Such strategies are the foundation for this book of six easy holiday menus, each of which has been specially created by an expert cook who has also contributed to other volumes of the Williams-Sonoma Kitchen Library. On the following pages, you'll find all the information you need to host a truly great holiday party, including a guide to serving pieces, a wealth of entertaining tips and, for each menu, detailed instructions on how to present it with style and ease.

Every one of the holiday menus includes some traditional favorites along with exciting new recipes; all of them feature the best, easiest-to-find ingredients of the season. As complete and helpful as the menus are, I'd also like to encourage you to change them as you wish, swapping dishes from one menu to another and adding your own favorites. In short, make them your own.

More important still, you don't even need a holiday to serve these menus. All of them work splendidly for nearly any dinner party or buffet. Try one of them the next time you entertain, and your guests will soon be saying that you have the magic to make an occasion truly festive.

Chuck Williams

EQUIPMENT

All-purpose serving pieces to meet the demands of sit-down dinners and buffets alike

Although some cooks may have the desire and the storage space to set aside special serving pieces just for holiday meals, the majority of us make do very well by using all-purpose items such as those shown here. It's a good idea to have on hand sturdy yet attractive dishes and accessories that will double for small dinner parties and large buffets. Some of these pieces have the added advantage of being able to go directly from the oven to the table, making service that much easier.

1. Place Mats
For more casual entertaining, woven or fabric place mats help define individual place settings, add color and texture to the decor and assist in cleanup.

2. Soup Plates
Shallow, wide-rimmed soup plates are attractive vessels for presenting broths and soups. May also be used for serving pasta, salad or stew.

3. Chargers and Plates
Large-diameter chargers remain at each place setting through most of a sit-down meal, providing a background upon which each individually plated course is set. They may also be used as large dinner plates. Smaller-diameter plates are used on top of the chargers.

4. Bread Basket
Baskets are traditionally used for holding breads at the table. This one is made of stoneware, which can be heated and keeps the bread warm throughout the meal.

5. Tureen
Large-capacity tureen with a ladle and platter base, for serving soups or stews.

6. Soup Bowls
Informal bowls for soups, stews or desserts.

7. Cups and Saucers
For serving coffee or tea.

8. Salt and Pepper Shakers
Allow guests to season individual portions to taste. At a formal dinner, tiny shakers like those shown here may appear at each place setting.

9. Sauceboat
With a pouring lip, for serving sauces, condiments, dressings and gravies.

10. Ramekins
Individual ovenproof porcelain dishes, for baking and serving custards, small soufflés and other desserts, as well as savory mousses and hors d'oeuvres.

11. Dessert Plates
Plates for serving desserts at a sit-down meal or a buffet.

12. Casual Napkins
Good-quality fabric napkins in an informal, attractive pattern, chosen to coordinate with serving dishes.

13. Pie Server
Flat utensil with serrated edge, for cutting and serving pie or cake.

14. Slotted Serving Spoon
Large-capacity spoon for serving vegetables and other side dishes without transferring too much sauce or liquid.

15. Carving Fork and Knife
Sturdy two-pronged fork steadies roasts while the long, sharp, flexible blade slices meats or cuts between poultry joints with ease.

16. Gratin Dish
Porcelain dish for baking gratins. Its shallowness and its broad surface area promote the formation of a golden crust.

17. Serving Platter
Large, oval platter for presenting roasts and for general use on buffet tables.

18. Formal Napkins
Good-quality white cotton napkins present a bright, crisp look for more formal occasions.

19. Cutlery
A basic set of sturdy, handsome cutlery, including salad and dinner forks, knives and soup and dessert spoons, fully serves the needs of any entertaining menu.

20. Covered Casserole
For baked main courses, dressings and other dishes. The porcelain dish shown here comes with a basketlike holder, allowing it to be placed directly on the table without harming wood surfaces.

21. Trivet
Choose sturdy metal, ceramic or thickly woven trivets to protect surfaces from hot serving dishes.

22. Serving Tray
Large, flat serving tray with handles enables easy transfer of glassware, dishes and foods to and from the kitchen.

23. Wine Glasses
For general entertaining, have on hand a set of reasonably priced, goblet-style all-purpose glasses in which both white and red wines—as well as water—can be served.

24. Decanters
Glass decanters for presenting wine at the table.

25. Covered Vegetable Dish
Shallow dish of porcelain (shown here), pottery, stoneware or other heat-retaining material keeps side dishes warm at the table.

26. Baking Dish
All-purpose, large-capacity baking dish may be used for preparing and serving appetizers, main courses, side dishes and desserts.

27. Salad Set
For tossing and serving salads, have on hand a large-capacity bowl and oversized spoon and fork. The matching serving bowls shown here may also be used for desserts.

Holiday Entertaining Tips

Any truly memorable holiday party—whether a sit-down dinner or a casual buffet—is the result of a dynamic combination of creativity, planning and organization. The creativity comes in the foods you choose to cook, the way you present them and how you set the scene. Planning and organization work hand in hand to make the event flow in a seemingly effortless manner, both for you and your guests.

✦ Planning ✦

Decide on the guest list and seating: Aim for a dynamic mix of people with complementary interests and personalities. Plan seating to spark lively conversation.

Issue the invitations: For traditional holidays, invite guests at least a month in advance. Invitations for informal gatherings may be extended by telephone. For more formal occasions, send written invitations, requesting an RSVP by phone or in writing.

Plan the menu: Before deciding on what to serve, consider the occasion and any traditional foods it might require, what ingredients are in season, and the special tastes or dietary needs of your guests.

Select the wines: Let the menu and your own and your guests' preferences determine what wines or other beverages you serve. Although red wines generally best complement meat and white wines fish, you could offer either a light red or a robust white with poultry, light meats like veal or pork, or rich seafood like lobster or salmon.

✦ Shopping & Cooking Ahead ✦

Double-check the recipes: Several days before the event, read all the recipes and make-ahead suggestions to ensure you have all ingredients needing advance preparation.

Prepare a shopping list: Based on ingredient lists, prepare a master shopping list divided, if necessary, into separate categories for items to be purchased in the food market, produce shop, butcher shop, wine shop and so on. Check the list against supplies in your refrigerator and pantry.

Make additional lists: Make separate lists of all the cookware, serving pieces and decorative items you need. Check off those you have on hand; buy, borrow or rent those you don't.

✦ Setting the Scene ✦

Decide on the setting: Although most parties will be held in the dining room, consider other settings such as a spacious kitchen, family room or den, or, if weather allows, a patio or garden.

Clean the house: Allow plenty of time to tidy your rooms. Make sure the guest bath is well stocked with hand towels, soaps and other supplies. Prepare a spot for storing coats.

Attend to seating: Make sure there's ample space in the dining area. Press into service chairs or tables from other rooms, or borrow or rent them.

Choose the tableware: If you have more than one set of dishes and serving pieces, select those whose shape, size, color and pattern will best complement the menu. Don't be afraid to mix and match.

Plan flowers and other centerpieces: Select relatively scent-free flowers and greenery that won't interfere with the food. Consider other decorative items such as shells and seasonal fruits and vegetables. Keep arrangements low, so that guests can converse easily across the table.

Plan the lighting: Supplement unscented, dripless candles with electric lighting to define conversation areas and keep the room from being too dark.

Select the music: Choose music to match the spirit and traditions of the occasion. Keep volume low.

✦ BUFFET TIPS ✦

Arrange the room thoughtfully: Survey the setting and consider rearranging the furniture so that separate tables or areas for food, drinks and seating are positioned to allow easy traffic flow and comfortable places for guests to gather.

Set up stations: Especially for large buffets, consider setting up separate tables for different courses—appetizers, main courses, desserts—so that guests

can serve themselves more comfortably at their own pace. Include ample supplies of plates, cutlery and napkins at each table.

Pay attention to temperatures: To keep hot foods hot, use chafing dishes and hot plates, borrowing or renting them if necessary. Depending upon the size of the party, prepare the food in batches, so you can present it freshly cooked.

✦ LITTLE THINGS THAT MAKE A BIG DIFFERENCE ✦

Keep a logbook: Every time you host a party, enter into the log such details as the guest list, seating, menu, successes and disappointments. Refer to the log when planning future parties.

Have a trial run: If any recipes seem at all challenging or unfamiliar, cook them for the family a week or more before the party.

Ask for help: If your own schedule or the size of the party makes entertaining seem daunting, enlist the aid of friends or family, or consider hiring temporary help.

Consider gifts and favors: Offer each guest a small memento—an instant photograph, a posy of flowers, a jar of homemade preserves or any other item that, although inexpensive, expresses thoughtfulness and appreciation.

Don't panic: Most mishaps—flowers that didn't arrive, a missing garnish—won't be noticed by your guests if you don't mention them. Relax and enjoy your party!

Thanksgiving Dinner

OYSTER CHOWDER

CITRUS-SCENTED ROAST TURKEY
WITH CRANBERRY SAUCE

CORN BREAD AND DRIED FRUIT DRESSING

MIXED ROASTED ROOT VEGETABLES

STIR-FRIED BRUSSELS SPROUTS
WITH MUSTARD AND LEMON

PUMPKIN-HAZELNUT CHIFFON PIE

SERVES 6–8

THANKSGIVING IS THE QUINTESSENTIAL AMERICAN HOLIDAY. DATING BACK TO EARLIEST COLONIAL TIMES, THIS HARVEST FESTIVAL GIVES US THE OPPORTUNITY TO EXPRESS OUR GRATITUDE FOR THE GOOD THINGS LIFE HAS BESTOWED UPON US—FOOD, OF COURSE, BUT ALSO OUR HEALTH, OUR PERSONAL ACCOMPLISHMENTS AND, MOST OF ALL, THE LOVE AND SUPPORT OF OUR FAMILY AND FRIENDS. THE MENU THAT FOLLOWS HAS ITS FOUNDATION IN LONGSTANDING THANKSGIVING TRADITIONS, WITH ITS OYSTERS, TURKEY, CRANBERRIES, CORN BREAD, ROOT VEGETABLES AND PUMPKIN. IN A SIMILARLY TRADITIONAL VEIN, WE SHOW IT SERVED IN A FAMILY DINING ROOM, WITH SETTINGS FEATURING SIMPLE TABLEWARE THAT EVOKE THE PAST. AN ASSORTMENT OF GOURDS AND OTHER EASILY MADE CENTERPIECES AND AUTUMN-LEAF PLACE CARDS CHARMINGLY ECHO THE HARVEST SEASON—AND PROVIDE LOVELY MEMENTOS FOR GUESTS TO CARRY HOME.

A seasonal place card welcomes each guest.

✦ MAKING AUTUMNAL PLACE CARDS ✦
To make place cards, cut out leaf shapes from autumnal-colored craft paper and write a guest's name on each leaf. Using wire ribbon, available in a florist's shop or craft store, secure each leaf to a small bundle of trimmed decorative branches, wheat shafts, evergreen sprigs or other hardy seasonal foliage.

✦ DRINK SUGGESTIONS ✦
Offer guests their choice of a full-bodied Chardonnay or, if they'd prefer red wine, a light Pinot Noir or Beaujolais Nouveau. With dessert, pour a sweet dessert wine such as a late-harvest Riesling; or pass a well-aged Cognac.

✥ PREPARATION STRATEGIES ✥

The night before: make the corn bread, then cut into cubes and leave to dry; make and refrigerate the pie.

Early morning: assemble the dressing; parboil the Brussels sprouts.

About 5 hours ahead: remove the turkey from the refrigerator to bring to room temperature.

About 4 hours ahead: start roasting the turkey; make the cranberry sauce.

About 1 hour ahead: prepare the root vegetables for baking; begin baking the dressing; whip the cream for the pie and chill.

About 30 minutes ahead: start cooking the oyster chowder; slip the root vegetables into the oven after removing the turkey.

Just before serving: stir-fry the Brussels sprouts.

✥ MAKING HOLIDAY TOPIARIES ✥

To assemble holiday topiaries for display on the dining table or on the mantel, begin by cutting off the heads of dried flower buds, seedpods or other compact decorative foliage. Use a glue gun or glue pot to attach them in concentric circles to a Styrofoam ball. When the ball is about two-thirds covered, secure its uncovered portion to a large square of sheet moss, using long pins. Tuck the moss into a small flowerpot to display the topiary ball.

Use a Styrofoam ball and decorative seedpods.

Trim the pods from their stems and glue to the ball.

The completed topiary, set in a flowerpot.

Oyster Chowder

2 tablespoons unsalted butter

4 slices bacon, coarsely chopped

1 small yellow onion, finely diced

1 celery stalk, thinly sliced

1 small carrot, peeled and finely diced

½ red bell pepper (capsicum), seeded, deribbed and finely diced

3 cups (24 fl oz/750 ml) heavy (double) cream

1 cup (8 fl oz/250 ml) dry white wine

salt and freshly ground pepper

36 small bottled shucked oysters with their liquor

2 tablespoons finely chopped fresh flat-leaf (Italian) parsley

2 teaspoons finely chopped fresh tarragon

Oysters were no doubt plentiful at the Pilgrims' first Thanksgiving dinner. This simple, quick soup shows them off in robust yet elegant fashion. For a lighter version, eliminate the bacon and substitute half-and-half (half cream) or milk for the cream. Chopped fresh chives can be used in place of the tarragon.

✛

*I*n a soup pot over medium heat, melt the butter. Add the bacon and sauté just until it begins to brown, 2–3 minutes. Using a slotted spoon, transfer to paper towels to drain. Set aside.

Pour off about half of the fat from the pot and return the pot to medium heat. Add the onion, celery, carrot and bell pepper. Stir well, cover, reduce the heat to low and cook, stirring occasionally, until the vegetables are soft, about 12 minutes.

Add the cream, wine, and salt and pepper to taste and raise the heat to medium. Heat just until bubbles appear around the edges of the pot. Reduce the heat to low, add the oysters and their liquor and the reserved bacon and simmer very gently until the oysters are cooked, 1–2 minutes; they should be slightly firm to the touch. Do not allow to boil. Stir in the parsley and tarragon.

Ladle into warmed bowls and serve immediately.

Serves 6–8

Citrus-Scented Roast Turkey with Cranberry Sauce

10–12 lb (5–6 kg) turkey, at room
   temperature
salt and freshly ground pepper
2 celery stalks, cut into 2-inch (5-cm)
   lengths
1 yellow onion, quartered
1 orange, quartered
1 lemon, quartered
1 bay leaf
3 fresh parsley sprigs
¼ cup (2 oz/60 g) unsalted butter, at
   room temperature
1 cup (8 fl oz/250 ml) chicken stock

FOR THE CRANBERRY SAUCE:
3 cups (12 oz/375 g) fresh or frozen
   whole cranberries
1 cup (8 oz/250 g) sugar
finely grated zest and juice of 1 orange
1 cup (8 fl oz/250 ml) water
1 cinnamon stick, about 3 inches (7.5 cm)
   long, broken in half
¼ teaspoon ground cloves
1 cup (4 oz/125 g) coarsely chopped
   walnuts, toasted (see glossary, page 106)
   (optional)

Position a rack in the middle of an oven and preheat to 425°F (220°C). Oil a V-shaped rack in a roasting pan.

Remove the neck, gizzard and heart from the turkey and discard or reserve for another use. Rinse with cold water, inside and out; pat dry with paper towels. Season the cavity with salt and pepper and place the celery, onion, orange, lemon, bay leaf and parsley in it. Truss the turkey, if desired. Rub the outside of the bird with the butter and sprinkle with salt and pepper.

Place on the rack in the pan, breast side down. Roast for 40 minutes, basting with the pan juices after 20 minutes. Add the chicken stock to the pan and reduce the heat to 325°F (165°C); turn breast-side up and continue to roast, basting every 15–20 minutes with the pan juices. Roast until golden and cooked through. After about 2 hours, start testing for doneness by inserting an instant-read thermometer into the thickest part of the breast away from the bone; it should register 165°F (74°C). Alternatively, insert it into the thickest part of the thigh; it should register 180°F (82°C). The turkey should roast a total of 2½–3¼ hours.

As soon as the turkey is in the oven, begin to make the cranberry sauce: Sort through the cranberries, discarding any soft ones. In a saucepan over medium-high heat, stir together the cranberries, sugar, orange zest and juice, water, cinnamon stick and cloves. Bring to a boil, reduce the heat to low and cover partially. Simmer gently, stirring occasionally, until the sauce thickens and most of the cranberries have burst, 10–15 minutes.

Transfer to a bowl and let cool, then cover and refrigerate until serving. Stir in the toasted walnuts (if using) just before serving. You will have about 4½ cups (36 fl oz/1.1 l) sauce.

Transfer the turkey to a warmed platter, cover loosely with aluminum foil and let rest for 20–30 minutes before carving. Serve the turkey with the cranberry sauce.

Serves 6–8 with leftovers

Corn Bread and Dried Fruit Dressing

FOR THE BASIC CORN BREAD:

1 cup (5 oz/155 g) yellow cornmeal

1 cup (5 oz/155 g) all-purpose (plain) flour

2 tablespoons sugar

1 tablespoon baking powder

½ teaspoon salt

2 eggs, lightly beaten

1 cup (8 fl oz/250 ml) nonfat milk

¼ cup (2 fl oz/60 ml) vegetable oil

FOR THE DRESSING MIXTURE:

½ cup (3 oz/90 g) seedless raisins

½ cup (3 oz/90 g) coarsely chopped dried apricots

1 cup (8 fl oz/250 ml) dry white wine

¼ cup (2 oz/60 g) unsalted butter

1 yellow onion, diced

1 clove garlic, minced

2 celery stalks, diced

1 small tart green apple, cored and diced

1 tablespoon crushed dried sage

2 cups (16 fl oz/500 ml) chicken stock

4 tablespoons chopped fresh parsley

1 cup (4½ oz/140 g) slivered almonds, toasted (*see glossary, page 106*)

salt and freshly ground pepper

*T*o make the corn bread, the day before, position a rack in the middle of an oven and preheat to 400°F (200°C). Lightly grease an 8-inch (20-cm) square baking pan.

In a bowl, stir together the cornmeal, flour, sugar, baking powder and salt. In another bowl, stir together the eggs, milk and vegetable oil until well blended. Pour the egg mixture into the cornmeal mixture and stir just until they form a smooth batter. Pour into the baking pan. Bake until golden brown and a toothpick inserted into the center comes out clean, about 30 minutes. Let cool in the pan on a rack for 10 minutes, then unmold and let cool to room temperature. Cut the bread in half horizontally, then cut into ½–1-inch (12-mm–2.5-cm) cubes. Spread on 2 baking sheets and let dry overnight at room temperature.

The next day, make the dressing mixture: Put the raisins and dried apricots in a bowl, pour in the wine and let stand to soak, about 30 minutes. Butter a 3-qt (3-l) baking dish.

In a large sauté pan or frying pan over medium heat, melt the butter. Add the onion and garlic and sauté, stirring, until translucent, 2–3 minutes. Add the celery, apple and sage and mix well. Sauté for another 2 minutes. Remove from the heat and set aside.

Put the bread cubes in a large bowl. Gradually add the stock, tossing to moisten evenly. Drain the soaked fruits and add to the bowl along with the sautéed vegetables, parsley, almonds, and salt and pepper to taste. Mix well until blended. Spoon the dressing loosely into the prepared dish. (The dressing can be assembled up to this point several hours in advance, covered and refrigerated.)

About 30 minutes before the turkey is done roasting, place the dressing on a rack in the lower third of the 325°F (165°C) oven. When the turkey has been removed, raise the oven temperature to 375°F (190°C) and continue baking until golden, 20–30 minutes longer. Serve immediately.

Serves 6–8

Mixed Roasted Root Vegetables

1 tablespoon salt, plus salt to taste

1 lb (500 g) white potatoes, well scrubbed
   and cut into 2-inch (5-cm) pieces

1 lb (500 g) carrots, well scrubbed and
   cut into 2-inch (5-cm) lengths

1 lb (500 g) parsnips, well scrubbed and
   cut into 2-inch (5-cm) pieces

2 tablespoons unsalted butter, melted

2 tablespoons olive oil

freshly ground pepper

2 tablespoons chopped fresh parsley

*Oven-roasted carrots and parsnips develop a rich, sweet flavor that
makes them worthy companions to the traditional roasted potatoes.
The vegetables can be left unpeeled, which gives them an appealing
knobby look and a better, crustier surface when cooked. For a slightly
more elegant dish, peel them. Have this vegetable mixture ready to go
into the oven the moment you remove the turkey.*

✣

*F*ill a large pot three-fourths full with water and bring to a boil.
Add the 1 tablespoon salt and the potatoes, carrots and parsnips.
Bring back to a boil, reduce the heat slightly, cover partially and
cook for 5 minutes. Drain well.

In a baking dish just large enough to hold the vegetables in a
single layer, toss the vegetables with the butter and olive oil, a
little more salt and pepper to taste. Set aside.

As soon as the turkey is done and has been removed from the
oven to rest before carving, raise the oven temperature to 375°F
(190°C) and roast the vegetables on the middle rack, turning
them several times, until tender and golden, 20–30 minutes.
(The dressing will be baking at the same time.)

Transfer to a serving dish, sprinkle with the parsley and serve.

Serves 6–8

Stir-fried Brussels Sprouts with Mustard and Lemon

1 teaspoon salt, plus salt to taste
1½ lb (750 g) Brussels sprouts, trimmed and cut lengthwise in halves
3 tablespoons fresh lemon juice
1½ tablespoons whole-grain mustard
3 tablespoons olive oil
freshly ground pepper

Mustard and lemon add sparkle to crisply cooked Brussels sprouts. If you prefer, substitute Savoy cabbage, cut into strips 1 inch (2.5 cm) wide; omit the parboiling.

Fill a large saucepan three-fourths full with water and bring to a boil. Add the 1 teaspoon salt and the Brussels sprouts and cook until tender but still crisp, 2–3 minutes. Drain the sprouts well and let cool to room temperature. (The Brussels sprouts can be parboiled up to several hours in advance, then covered and refrigerated.)

In a bowl, stir together the lemon juice and mustard. Set aside.

Shortly before serving time, heat the olive oil in a large wok or heavy frying pan over medium-high heat. Add the Brussels sprouts and stir-fry until their edges just begin to turn golden, 1–2 minutes. At the last moment, add the lemon juice–mustard mixture and stir briskly to coat the sprouts. Season to taste with salt and pepper.

Transfer to a warmed bowl and serve at once.

Serves 6–8

Pumpkin-Hazelnut Chiffon Pie

FOR THE GINGERSNAP-HAZELNUT CRUST:

1¼ cups (6½ oz/200 g) gingersnap
    crumbs
¼ cup (1 oz/30 g) lightly toasted, peeled
    and finely chopped hazelnuts (filberts)
    (*see glossary, page 106*)
2 tablespoons sugar
pinch of salt
½ cup (4 oz/125 g) unsalted butter,
    melted

FOR THE CHIFFON FILLING:

1 tablespoon unflavored gelatin
¼ cup (2 fl oz/60 ml) water
3 eggs, separated, at room temperature
1½ cups (12 oz/375 g) canned solid-pack
    pumpkin
¾ cup (6 oz/185 g) firmly packed golden
    brown sugar
½ cup (4 fl oz/125 ml) half-and-half
1 teaspoon ground cinnamon
½ teaspoon ground ginger
½ teaspoon freshly grated nutmeg
½ teaspoon ground allspice
½ teaspoon salt
ice cubes
1 tablespoon granulated sugar
2 tablespoons Frangelico
¾ cup (6 fl oz/180 ml) heavy (double)
    cream, lightly whipped, chilled
    (optional)

To make the crust: Position a rack in the middle of an oven and preheat to 325°F (165°C). Combine the gingersnap crumbs, hazelnuts, sugar and salt in a bowl and toss together. Add the melted butter and stir vigorously until blended.

Using your fingers, press and pat the mixture over the bottom and up the sides of a 9-inch (23-cm) pie pan, extending the sides about ¼ inch (6 mm) above the rim (the crust will shrink slightly in baking) and taking care not to make them too thick. Bake for 8 minutes, then set aside on a rack to cool completely.

To make the filling: In a small bowl, stir together the gelatin and water. Set aside to let the gelatin soften. Place the egg yolks in a heatproof bowl or in the top pan of a double boiler, away from the heat, and beat lightly. Stir in the pumpkin, brown sugar, half-and-half, cinnamon, ginger, nutmeg, allspice and salt until well blended. Set over a pan of gently simmering water but not touching the water. Cook, stirring constantly with a wire whisk, until the mixture is hot and thick enough to hold a peak when the whisk is lifted out, about 15 minutes. Remove from the heat and stir in the softened gelatin. Place the bottom of the bowl or pan in a baking pan filled with ice cubes and water and stir constantly until the mixture is completely cooled, about 15 minutes. Set aside.

In a bowl, using an electric mixer set on medium speed, beat the egg whites until frothy. Sprinkle in the granulated sugar and continue beating until the whites are stiff enough to hold firm peaks when the beaters are lifted. Using a rubber spatula, gently fold the egg whites and the Frangelico into the pumpkin mixture until thoroughly blended.

Transfer the filling to the baked pie crust, using the rubber spatula to smooth and mound its surface. Refrigerate for at least 2 hours to set.

Cut into wedges and serve chilled, accompanied with whipped cream, if you like.

Makes one 9-inch (23-cm) pie; serves 6–8

Hanukkah Dinner

MILLIE'S HERRING SALAD

SWEET-AND-SOUR BRISKET

POTATO LATKES

APPLESAUCE

DORA APTER'S MANDLEBREAD

DRIED FRUIT COMPOTE

SERVES 8

Millie's Herring Salad

1 jar (32 oz/1 kg) herring snacks
1 day-old roll or 1 slice white bread
¼ cup (2 fl oz/60 ml) cider vinegar
1 yellow onion, cut into large chunks
1 large celery stalk, cut into 1-inch
   (2.5-cm) pieces
1 Granny Smith or other firm, tart apple,
   peeled, quartered and cored
1 hard-cooked egg, quartered
1 tablespoon sugar
crackers or thinly sliced pumpernickel
   bread

Your family and friends will find this easy-to-make appetizer completely irresistible. Take care not to overblend; you don't want the mixture to lose its personality. Look for herring snacks (marinated herring pieces) in jars in the refrigerated case of food stores and delicatessens. The salad can be made up to 3 days in advance, tightly covered and refrigerated. Bring to room temperature before serving.

>‹

*E*mpty the herring into a sieve to drain; discard the juice. Break the roll or bread into several pieces, place in a small bowl and sprinkle on the vinegar. Set aside.

In a food processor fitted with the metal blade, combine the onion, celery and apple. Using on-off pulses of 2 or 3 seconds, process until coarsely chopped. Add the egg and process for 5 seconds. Then add the herring, the roll or bread (and any unabsorbed vinegar) and the sugar. Using on-off pulses, process until the ingredients are incorporated but not puréed. The consistency should be coarse.

Transfer to a serving bowl and serve immediately with crackers or pumpernickel bread.

Serves 8

Sweet-and-Sour Brisket

1 brisket, 5–6 lb (2.5–3 kg), or 2 smaller
   pieces of equal weight

¼ cup (2 fl oz/60 ml) water

2 large yellow onions, cut into slices
   ½ inch (12 mm) thick

4 large celery stalks, including leaves,
   cut into slices ½ inch (12 mm) thick

1 bottle (8 fl oz/250 ml) chili sauce or
   spicy catsup

4 large cloves garlic, chopped

2 bay leaves

½ cup (3½ oz/105 g) firmly packed dark
   brown sugar

⅓ cup (2½ oz/75 g) Dijon mustard

¼ cup (2 fl oz/60 ml) soy sauce

¼ cup (2 fl oz/60 ml) red wine vinegar

3 tablespoons molasses

1 bottle (12 fl oz/375 ml) beer

½ teaspoon paprika

4 large baking potatoes, peeled and cut
   into slices 1 inch (2.5 cm) thick

salt and freshly ground pepper

This mouth-watering dish can be simmered on top of the stove or cooked in a crockpot. It can be made 3 days in advance and refrigerated, or frozen for up to 6 months (slice it before wrapping for freezing).

>‹

*I*n a Dutch oven or other heavy pot over medium heat, sear the meat, fat side down, for 5–10 minutes. When it begins to brown, turn and brown the other side, 5–10 minutes longer. Remove the brisket from the pot. Using a large spoon, skim off any fat from the drippings and discard, but leave the drippings in the pot.

Add the water, onions, celery, chili sauce, garlic, bay leaves, brown sugar, mustard, soy sauce, vinegar and molasses to the pot and stir to mix well. Return the brisket to the pot, cover and cook over medium-low heat for 3 hours. Add the beer, paprika and potatoes. Re-cover and continue to cook for 1 hour longer. Add water, if necessary, to keep the mixture moist.

To cook the brisket in a crockpot: Sear the meat on the stove top as directed, then place all the ingredients except the salt and pepper in a large crockpot set on high. Cover and cook until the meat is very tender, 6–8 hours.

Allow the brisket to cool in the liquid for 30 minutes, then transfer it to a container. Pour the cooking liquid and potatoes into a bowl. Discard the bay leaves. Let the liquid and meat cool for at least 2 hours, then skim off the fat from the liquid. Return the liquid and potatoes to a heavy pot with a lid.

Cut the meat across the grain into slices ¼ inch (6 mm) thick and add it to the liquid. Cover and reheat the meat and potatoes over low heat. (Alternatively, reheat in a covered container in a microwave oven.) Season to taste with salt and pepper.

To serve, arrange the slices on a large warmed platter. Surround or top with the cooking liquid and potatoes.

Serves 8

Potato Latkes

ice water
6 large baking potatoes, 2½–3 lb
   (1.25–1.5 kg), well scrubbed and cut
   into pieces 2 inches (5 cm) thick
2 yellow onions, quartered
2 extra-large eggs
½ cup (2½ oz/75 g) all-purpose (plain)
   flour
½ teaspoon baking soda (bicarbonate
   of soda)
1 tablespoon salt
2 teaspoons freshly ground pepper
vegetable oil for frying

You may peel the potatoes if you prefer, but the peel imparts extra texture and flavor to the latkes. *The cooked* latkes *can be placed between layers of plastic wrap on a baking sheet and refrigerated for up to 1 day, or they can be frozen, transferred to freezer bags and stored in the freezer for up to 3 months. Reheat in a 350°F (180°C) oven for about 15 minutes.*

✦

*H*ave ready a large metal bowl filled with ice water. In a food processor fitted with the coarse grating blade, grate the potatoes in 3 batches (or use a hand grater). Transfer them to the bowl of ice water. Refrigerate for 2–3 hours, changing the water twice during that time. Grate the onions and set them aside.

Empty the potatoes into a large sieve or colander and, using your hands, press out as much water as possible. In a large bowl, combine the potatoes and onions and mix well. In a small bowl, beat the eggs until blended. In another small bowl, stir together the flour and baking soda. Stir the eggs and the flour mixture into the potatoes and then stir in the salt and pepper.

Preheat an oven to 200°F (95°C).

In a large frying pan or griddle over high heat or an electric frying pan set at 400°F (200°C), pour in vegetable oil to a depth of ¼ inch (6 mm). When the oil is hot enough to make a drop of water sizzle, spoon mounds of batter about 2½ inches (6 cm) in diameter into the oil, being careful not to crowd the pan. Flatten the tops slightly with a spatula and fry until the undersides are brown and crisp, about 4 minutes. Carefully turn the *latkes* and cook the second side until brown, about 4 minutes longer. Using a slotted metal spatula, transfer the latkes to a baking sheet lined with paper towels to drain. Cover the baking sheet loosely with foil and place in the oven until all the batter has been cooked.

Arrange on a platter and serve hot with applesauce (page 36).

Serves 8

Applesauce

8–10 large, sweet, flavorful apples such as Rome, Baldwin or McIntosh, 2–3 lb (2–2.5 kg) total weight, quartered and cored

1½ cups (12 fl oz/375 ml) water or apple cider

½ teaspoon ground cinnamon

¾–1 cup (6–8 oz/185–250 g) sugar

fresh lemon juice

When you see how easy it is to make homemade applesauce, you'll never settle for store-bought again. The applesauce can be stored in the refrigerator for up to 1 week or in the freezer for up to 6 months.

✢✢

Peel the apples (you can leave the peels on if you will be puréeing the apples in a food mill). Combine the apples with the water or cider in a deep, heavy-bottomed pot over low heat. Cook, stirring once or twice, until the apples are very tender, 20–30 minutes.

Drain the apples, reserving the liquid. Pass the apples through a food mill, adding the cinnamon, sugar and lemon juice to taste and ⅓–½ cup (3–4 fl oz/80–125 ml) of the cooking liquid, or as needed to achieve a good consistency. Alternatively, purée the apples in a food processor fitted with the metal blade, adding the remaining ingredients during processing.

Transfer to a bowl and serve with potato *latkes* (page 35).

Serves 8

Dora Apter's Mandlebread

These homey cookies, loaded with nuts, are slightly chewier than Italian biscotti but still stand up to a dunk in a cup of coffee or tea.

>+<

1 generous cup (5 oz/155 g) whole hazelnuts (filberts) or almonds, or a mixture
4 extra-large eggs
1 cup (8 oz/250 g) sugar
1 cup (8 fl oz/250 ml) vegetable oil
4 cups (1 lb/500 g) all-purpose (plain)
   flour, sifted before measuring, plus
   extra if needed for kneading
1 teaspoon salt
4 teaspoons baking soda (bicarbonate
   of soda)
2 teaspoons almond extract (essence)
⅔ cup (5 oz/155 g) sugar mixed with
   3 tablespoons ground cinnamon
1 egg, lightly beaten with 1 tablespoon
   water

*P*osition 2 racks in the middle of an oven and preheat to 350°F (180°C). Line 2 baking sheets with aluminum foil.

If using hazelnuts, toast and then remove skins (see glossary, page 106). Set aside.

In a large bowl, using an electric mixer set on high speed, beat together the 4 eggs and 1 cup (8 oz/250 g) sugar until light and fluffy, about 3 minutes. Reduce the speed to low and beat in the oil just until incorporated. In another bowl, sift together the flour, salt and baking soda. With the mixer set on low speed, add the flour mixture to the egg mixture, beating only until incorporated. Mix in the almond extract and hazelnuts and/or almonds.

Turn out the dough onto a floured work surface. Adding a little flour if the dough is very sticky, knead 5 or 6 turns until a ball forms. Divide into 5 equal pieces. Knead 1 tablespoon of the cinnamon sugar into each piece, then form into flat logs 12 inches (30 cm) long and 2 inches (5 cm) wide. Carefully transfer the logs to the prepared sheets, spacing them 3 inches (7.5 cm) apart. Brush the tops with the egg-water mixture, then sprinkle with the remaining cinnamon sugar mixture.

Bake until the tops are dry and slightly cracked, about 30 minutes. At the halfway point, switch the baking sheets between the shelves, turning them 180 degrees as well. Transfer the logs to a work surface. Using a serrated knife, cut crosswise into slices 1½ inches (4 cm) wide. Place the slices on the baking sheets, cut sides down. Return them to the oven until lightly golden brown, 4–5 minutes. Turn the cookies over and bake until lightly browned on the second side. Let cool completely on wire racks. Store airtight for up to 2 weeks at room temperature.

Makes about 4 dozen

Dried Fruit Compote

4 cups (1½ lb/750 g) mixed dried fruits such as pitted prunes, apples, peaches, apricots, pears, figs and cherries, in any combination

½ cup (3 oz/90 g) golden raisins (sultanas)

1⅓ cups (11 fl oz/340 ml) sweet Marsala wine

2 cups (16 fl oz/500 ml) fresh orange juice

1 cup (8 fl oz/250 ml) water

1 cinnamon stick, about 3 inches (7.5 cm) long

Dried fruits have an intensity of flavor that makes this compote a wonderful finish to a holiday meal. For an alcohol-free version, omit the Marsala and increase the orange juice to 3⅓ cups (27 fl oz/840 ml). The compote can be made up to 4 weeks in advance and stored tightly covered in the refrigerator.

✈

*I*n a large, heavy-bottomed pot over medium heat, combine all of the ingredients. Cover and when the liquid starts to simmer, reduce the heat to low and cook, stirring gently once or twice, until the fruit is quite soft but not disintegrated, about 30 minutes.

Remove from the heat and let cool to room temperature. Remove the cinnamon stick and discard. Transfer to a glass serving bowl and serve warm. Or the compote may be covered and refrigerated; let it come to room temperature before serving.

Serves 8

Holiday Open House

Smoked Salmon on Potatoes
with Dill Sauce

Red, White and Green Toasts

Holiday Ham Platter

Green Bean, Radicchio and Fennel Salad

Wild Rice, Orange and Asparagus Salad

Cardamom Molasses Spice Cookies

SERVES 24

Crown-shaped spice cookies, fresh from the oven, coated with white icing . . .

. . . and decorated with a holiday plaid of red and green stripes.

❖ DECORATING HOLIDAY COOKIES ❖

The cardamom molasses spice cookies included in this menu (page 56) are easily transformed into festive decorations in their own right. After the dough has been mixed and rolled out, use decorative cutters to shape the cookies. Once they have been baked and then cooled, spread them with the white icing included in the recipe. Mix separate, smaller batches of icing and tint them with different food colorings. Then use a pastry bag fitted with a small tip to apply the colored icing to the hardened white base. A plastic bag with a hole snipped in the corner also works well; or simply drizzle the colored icing from the tip of a small spoon.

A T NO TIME OF YEAR ARE FRIENDS AND RELATIONS MORE LIKELY TO STOP BY THAN DURING THE HOLIDAYS. AN OPEN-HOUSE BUFFET SUCH AS THE ONE PRESENTED HERE IS THE PERFECT WAY TO WELCOME THOSE GUESTS, ALLOWING THEM TO SERVE THEMSELVES AND LEAVING YOU MORE TIME TO ENJOY THE PARTY. THE FULLY BAKED HAM THAT IS THE MAIN ATTRACTION OF OUR HOLIDAY BUFFET KEEPS WELL ON THE TABLE; BECAUSE IT IS SPIRAL CUT, SELF-SERVICE IS EXCEPTIONALLY SIMPLE. TO MAKE THE PARTY ALL THE EASIER, WE KEPT DECORATIONS TO A MINIMUM, LETTING LINENS IN A BRIGHT SEASONAL RED COMPLEMENT COLORFUL RIBBONS, BEESWAX CANDLES AND TRADITIONAL GREENERY. WE ALSO FOUND A NOVEL WAY TO KEEP WINES CHILLED AND CLOSE AT HAND (RIGHT). THE COOKIES THAT CONCLUDE THE MENU WILL ADD THEIR OWN FESTIVE TOUCH IF YOU MAKE THE EXTRA EFFORT TO CUT AND DECORATE THEM IN HOLIDAY SHAPES AND PATTERNS.

✤ DRINK SUGGESTIONS ✦

On a chilly day, serve red wine or cider mulled with sweet spices and sugar or honey over gentle heat. Offer guests the alternative of white wine, allowing them to serve themselves (see below).

✤ PREPARATION STRATEGIES ✦

Up to 4 days ahead: bake and decorate the cookies.

Up to 3 days ahead: prepare and refrigerate the sauces for the ham.

Up to 2 days ahead: prepare and refrigerate the topping for the toasts.

Up to 1 day ahead: toast the bread and store at room temperature; prepare and refrigerate ingredients for the salads.

About 4 hours ahead: prepare and refrigerate the dill sauce; prebake the potato slices.

About 2 hours ahead: assemble the toasts.

✤ SETTING UP A WINE COOLER ✦

When serving white wines or Champagne with a buffet, a single wine bucket is not large enough to keep all the drinks cold—especially when guests show up with their own contributions. Any good-sized, wide container such as a planter or wash basin can be pressed into service, however, by filling it with ice into which several bottles may be nestled. For a more festive look, tie ribbons around the container and surround it with greenery and pine cones. Arrange wine glasses nearby for guests to serve themselves.

A large basin becomes a holiday wine bucket.

Smoked Salmon on Potatoes with Dill Sauce

2 cups (16 fl oz/500 ml) sour cream

1 cup (1½ oz/45 g) minced fresh dill, plus tiny dill sprigs for garnish

¼ cup (2 oz/60 g) Dijon mustard

¼ cup (2 oz/60 g) firmly packed golden brown sugar

3 lb (1.5 kg) baby new potatoes, unpeeled and cut into slices ½ inch (12 mm) thick

6 tablespoons (3 fl oz/90 ml) olive oil

2 tablespoons finely grated lemon zest

salt and freshly ground pepper

1 lb (500 g) thinly sliced smoked salmon, cut into ¾–1-inch (2–2.5-cm) squares

The components for this elegant finger food can be prepared ahead. Reheat about one-fourth of the potato slices at a time, then top them, arrange them on a platter and set out on the buffet. Refill the platter as needed. Tiny bay shrimp make a tasty alternative to the salmon.

✦

*I*n a small bowl, stir together the sour cream, minced dill, mustard and brown sugar until well blended. Cover and refrigerate until well chilled.

Preheat an oven to 400°F (200°C).

In a large bowl, combine the potato slices, olive oil and lemon zest. Season generously with salt and pepper. Using a rubber spatula or your hands, turn the potato slices to coat them evenly with the oil and seasonings. Spread the slices in a single layer on large baking sheets. Bake, turning once, until golden brown on both sides and tender when pierced with the tip of a knife, about 15 minutes per side. (The potatoes can be prepared up to this point 4 hours in advance. Let cool completely, cover and store at room temperature. Before serving, reheat, uncovered, in a 375°F/190°C oven for 5 minutes.)

Place a dollop of the dill sauce atop each hot potato slice. Top each with 1 salmon piece and garnish with a dill sprig. Arrange on a warmed platter and serve.

Makes about 100 slices; serves 24

Red, White and Green Toasts

3 tablespoons olive oil, plus extra for brushing

4 yellow onions, halved and sliced

2 large red bell peppers (capsicums), seeded, deribbed, thinly sliced length-wise and slices cut crosswise into pieces 1 inch (2.5 cm) long

1 tablespoon plus 1 teaspoon chopped fresh rosemary, plus rosemary sprigs for garnish

1 teaspoon sugar

1 tablespoon sherry wine vinegar

salt and freshly ground pepper

1½ lb (750 g) French baguettes, cut into slices ½ inch (12 mm) thick (about 72 slices)

⅔ lb (315 g) blue cheese, crumbled

12 green (spring) onions, including tender green tops, sliced

Assemble these holiday nibbles before your guests arrive, then bake about one-fourth of them at a time. Use any good-quality blue cheese; Stilton would be a nice choice.

➤✦

*I*n a large, heavy frying pan over medium-high heat, warm the 3 tablespoons olive oil. Add the yellow onions and sauté until translucent, about 10 minutes. Add the bell peppers and chopped rosemary and sauté until the onions are soft, about 10 minutes longer. Add the sugar and vinegar and stir for 2 minutes. Remove from the heat. Season to taste with salt and pepper. (The recipe can be prepared up to this point 2 days in advance; cover and refrigerate.)

Preheat an oven to 375°F (190°C). Arrange the bread slices in a single layer on large baking sheets. Bake until golden brown on top, about 5 minutes. Remove from the oven. (The slices can be toasted up to 1 day in advance. Let cool completely, wrap tightly and store at room temperature; then return them to the baking sheets, browned side up, before continuing.)

Brush the browned tops with olive oil and sprinkle with pepper. Spoon the onion mixture atop the bread slices, dividing it evenly. Sprinkle the cheese evenly over the tops. (The recipe can be prepared up to this point 2 hours in advance. Cover and let stand at room temperature.)

Reduce the oven temperature to 350°F (180°C). Bake until the onion mixture is hot and the cheese is melted, about 5 minutes. Sprinkle the green onions atop the toasts. Transfer to a warmed platter, garnish with rosemary sprigs and serve.

Makes about 72 toasts; serves 24

Holiday Ham Platter

FOR THE CRANBERRY-HORSERADISH SAUCE:
2 packages (12 oz/375 g each) fresh cranberries (about 6 cups)
2 cups (1 lb/500 g) sugar
1½ cups (12 fl oz/375 ml) fresh orange
juice
⅓ cup (2½ oz/75 g) prepared horseradish
½ teaspoon ground cloves

FOR THE ARUGULA AND MUSTARD MAYONNAISE:
3 cups (24 fl oz/750 ml) mayonnaise
3 cups (4½ oz/140 g) chopped arugula
(rocket)
¼ cup (2 oz/60 g) Dijon mustard
¼ cup (2 fl oz/60 ml) fresh lemon juice
1½ teaspoons freshly ground pepper

ornamental or regular kale
1 fully baked ham, preferably honey
glazed and spiral cut (see note),
about 14 lb (7 kg)
Lady apples or other small red-and-yellow-
skinned apples
assorted breads and rolls

A purchased fully baked ham stars in this festive but simple-to-assemble menu. Look for one that is spiral cut (presliced) to make serving easier. Buy prepared horseradish from the refrigerated case if possible, as it has a fresh, strong flavor. The cranberry-horseradish sauce and the arugula and mustard mayonnaise can be prepared up to 3 days in advance, covered and refrigerated. A smoked turkey could replace the ham.

✷

To make the cranberry-horseradish sauce: Sort through the cran-berries and discard any soft ones. In a large, heavy saucepan over medium-high heat, combine the sugar and orange juice. Bring to a boil, stirring until the sugar dissolves. Add the cranberries and return to a boil. Reduce the heat to medium and simmer, stirring occasionally, until the cranberries begin to burst, about 8 minutes. Remove from the heat and let cool completely.

Mix in the horseradish and cloves and transfer to a bowl. Cover and refrigerate until well chilled. You will have about 4½ cups (36 fl oz/1.1 l).

To make the mayonnaise: In a food processor fitted with the metal blade, combine the mayonnaise, arugula, mustard, lemon juice and pepper. Process until the arugula is finely chopped and the mixture is well blended. Transfer to a bowl, cover and refrig-erate until needed. You will have about 4½ cups (36 fl oz/1.1 l).

Line a platter with the kale. Top with the ham and garnish the platter with the apples. Set bowls of the cranberry-horseradish sauce and the arugula and mustard mayonnaise and baskets of breads and rolls alongside the platter.

Serves 24

Green Bean, Radicchio and Fennel Salad

3 lb (1.5 kg) green beans, trimmed
salt
2¾ lb (1.4 kg) fennel bulbs
2 heads radicchio (red chicory), 1½ lb
  (750 g) total weight, halved, cored
  and sliced lengthwise
1 cup (8 fl oz/250 ml) plus 2 tablespoons
  olive oil
6 tablespoons (3 fl oz/90 ml) balsamic
  vinegar
3½ cups (14 oz/435 g) coarsely grated
  Parmesan cheese
freshly ground pepper

This is a zesty and crisp salad that holds up well on a buffet. You can save time on the day of the party by preparing the vegetables a day ahead and refrigerating them, then dressing the salad just before serving.

✦✦

*F*ill a large pot three-fourths full with water and bring to a boil. Add the green beans and salt to taste and boil until just tender-crisp, about 8 minutes. Drain and rinse under cold water to cool. Drain well. Transfer to a large bowl.

Trim off the tops from the fennel bulbs. Cut away any bruised areas on the bulbs and then cut into quarters lengthwise. Cut away the cores and slice the quarters lengthwise. Add the fennel and radicchio to the beans. (The recipe can be prepared up to this point 1 day in advance; cover and refrigerate.)

Pour the olive oil over the vegetables and toss to coat. Add the vinegar and toss to coat again. Add 3 cups (12 oz/375 g) of the cheese and salt and pepper to taste and mix well.

Transfer to a serving bowl. Sprinkle with the remaining ½ cup (2 oz/60 g) cheese and serve.

Serves 24

Wild Rice, Orange and Asparagus Salad

2⅔ cups (1 lb/500 g) wild rice
3 qt (3 l) water
salt
4 lb (2 kg) thin asparagus
⅔ cup (5 fl oz/160 ml) fresh orange juice
¼ cup (2 fl oz/60 ml) sherry wine vinegar
   or red wine vinegar
⅔ cup (5 fl oz/160 ml) olive oil
3 tablespoons grated orange zest
⅓ cup (½ oz/15 g) chopped fresh
   tarragon
freshly ground pepper
4 navel oranges
8 green (spring) onions, chopped
2 cups (8 oz/250 g) coarsely chopped
   pecans
2 heads romaine (cos) lettuce, cored
   and separated into leaves

Mix up this tasty salad the night before the gathering, then add the oranges, pecans and green onions just before serving. If asparagus is unavailable, broccoli florets or Belgian endive (chicory/witloof) can be used instead.

✦✦

Rinse the rice well with cool water, then drain well. Place in a large pot and add the 3 qt (3 l) water. Season to taste with salt and bring to a boil. Reduce the heat to low, cover and simmer until the rice is tender, about 40 minutes. Drain the rice well and transfer to a large bowl.

Meanwhile, using a sharp knife, cut off the tough ends of the asparagus and discard. Then cut off the tips and reserve. Cut the stalks crosswise into slices ½ inch (12 mm) long. Fill a large saucepan three-fourths full with water and bring to a boil. Add the asparagus tips and stalks and salt to taste and cook until tender-crisp, about 8 minutes. Drain and rinse under cold water to cool. Drain well. Add to the rice.

In a bowl, combine the orange juice and vinegar. Mix in the olive oil, orange zest and tarragon. Add to the rice and mix well. Season to taste with salt and pepper. (The recipe can be prepared up to this point 1 day in advance; cover and refrigerate.)

Peel the oranges, cutting away all of the white pith. Cut the oranges in half through their stem ends and remove any white membrane on the cut surfaces, then chop the pulp. Add the chopped oranges, green onions and pecans to the salad and mix well.

Line a large bowl with the romaine leaves. Spoon the salad into the bowl and serve.

Serves 24

Cardamom Molasses Spice Cookies

1 cup (4 oz/125 g) walnuts

4 cups (1¼ lb/625 g) all-purpose (plain) flour

1½ cups (10½ oz/330 g) firmly packed dark brown sugar

1 tablespoon ground cardamom

1 tablespoon ground ginger

2 teaspoons ground cinnamon

1 teaspoon salt

1 teaspoon baking soda (bicarbonate of soda)

½ cup (4 oz/125 g) unsalted butter, at room temperature

½ cup (4 oz/125 g) vegetable shortening, at room temperature

½ cup (4 fl oz/125 ml) dark molasses

2 eggs

1 tablespoon plus 1 teaspoon vanilla extract (essence)

2 tablespoons finely grated orange zest

FOR THE CONFECTIONERS' SUGAR ICING:

6 cups (1½ lb/750 g) confectioners' (icing) sugar

¼ cup (2 fl oz/60 ml) milk, or as needed

3 tablespoons fresh lemon juice

colored sugar crystals, optional

Place the walnuts in a food processor fitted with the metal blade and process to grind finely (do not process to a paste). Add ½ cup (2½ oz/75 g) of the flour and ½ cup (3½ oz/105 g) of the brown sugar and process to a powder; set aside.

In a bowl, sift together the remaining 3½ cups (17½ oz/550 g) flour, the spices, salt and baking soda; set aside. In a large bowl, combine the butter, shortening and the remaining 1 cup (7 oz/ 225 g) brown sugar. Using an electric mixer set on high speed, beat until light and fluffy, about 3 minutes. Add the molasses, eggs, vanilla and orange zest and again beat until light and fluffy. Add the flour and nut mixtures and beat on low speed just until incorporated. Gather into a ball, form into 4 disks, wrap separately and chill for at least 1 hour or up to 2 days.

Position 1 rack in the upper third of an oven and another in the middle; preheat to 350°F (180°C). Butter 2 baking sheets. Dust 1 disk with flour and place between 2 sheets of waxed paper. Roll out ¼ inch (6 mm) thick. Using decoratively shaped cutters about 2 inches (5 cm) in diameter, cut out cookies. Transfer to the prepared sheets, spacing them ½ inch (12 mm) apart. Chill any scraps.

Bake until firm on the edges and browned on the bottom, about 10 minutes. Let cool on wire racks. Repeat with the remaining dough and scraps.

Meanwhile, to make the icing, stir together all the ingredients until smooth. If the mixture is too thick to pipe or spread, thin with a little more milk.

Spread or pipe the icing onto the cooled cookies. (To make the plaid pattern shown here, see page 44.) Sprinkle with sugar crystals, if desired. Let stand until the icing sets, about 2 hours. Store airtight for up to 4 days at room temperature.

Makes about 6 dozen

Christmas Dinner

Blood Oranges and Celery Root
with Mustard Vinaigrette

Roast Pork Loin and Onions

Brown Rice Pilaf with Pecans

Broccoli and Mushrooms with Lemon

Ginger Steamed Pudding

SERVES 6

*Ribbons and fruit clusters
complement bright holiday
papers.*

✣ HOLIDAY GIFT EMBELLISHMENTS ✤
To add an extra flourish to holiday
presents, secure their ribbons with
clusters of tiny artificial fruits and
nuts. The festive embellishments
are available in millinery, craft and
decorations shops.

Most families justly regard Christmas dinner as the most important, most festive meal of the year. Yet, in today's hectic world, many of us are hard-pressed to produce this favorite meal in all its traditional splendor. Recognizing that fact, our menu forges convenient new traditions. Instead of roast poultry that can take hours to prepare, it features a delicious loin of pork that, complete with golden onions and sauce, is ready to serve in well under 1½ hours. Our dessert maintains strong ties to the past with steamed pudding, an old English holiday classic that is also surprisingly easy to make. Regardless of how quickly it goes together, this menu—more than any other meal you serve during the year—calls for your finest china and silver. Even the most modest settings can be made wonderfully festive when complemented with topiary-style holly trees.

✤ DRINK SUGGESTIONS ✤

The main course of pork goes well with either a robust white wine such as a Chardonnay or a light, fresh red such as a Pinot Noir or Beaujolais. Offer tea and coffee with the steamed pudding.

✤ PREPARATION STRATEGIES ✤

Up to 3 hours ahead: prepare and refrigerate the blood oranges and the lettuces and their dressing separately.

About 2 hours ahead: start preparing the pudding; start cooking the rice pilaf, then keep it warm over a pan of hot water.

About 1½ hours ahead: begin roasting the pork; cut up the broccoli and slice the mushrooms.

About 1 hour ahead: prepare the celery root for the salad; whip the cream for the pudding and refrigerate.

Holly trees are easy-to-make holiday decorations.

✤ MAKE YOUR OWN HOLLY TREES ✤

Miniature holly "trees" are easily made for decorating the Christmas dinner table, or for bringing a touch of the holidays to your living room mantel, coffee table or any other spot that strikes your fancy. Begin by filling a flowerpot with sheet moss. Insert a sturdy stick halfway into the base of a Styrofoam cone, available in a florist or craft shop. Anchor the cone atop the moss. Clip attractive leaves from sprays of holly and, using a glue gun or glue pot, attach the leaves to the cone, starting at its base and overlapping them in a circular pattern. Crown the top of the holly tree with a cluster of bright red holly berries.

Blood Oranges and Celery Root with Mustard Vinaigrette

3 blood oranges
1 tablespoon fruit-flavored vinegar, such as peach or raspberry, or mild white wine vinegar
⅛ teaspoon salt
freshly ground pepper
2 teaspoons Dijon mustard
2 teaspoons honey
⅓ cup (3 fl oz/80 ml) extra-virgin olive oil
1 celery root (celeriac), about 1 lb (500 g)
8–10 oz (250–315 g) mixed salad greens or a mixture of romaine (cos) and butter (Boston) lettuce and chicory (curly endive)

Blood oranges and celery root are found in the market in the cool months, making this an ideal first course for a Christmas meal. You may, however, use regular seedless oranges and fresh fennel in their place. If you use fennel, chop the bulbs coarsely. The oranges, vinaigrette and lettuces can be prepared up to 3 hours in advance and refrigerated separately.

➤←

Peel the oranges, cutting away all of the white pith and outer membrane. Holding each orange over a bowl and using a sharp, thin-bladed knife, cut along both sides of each segment, against the membranes, to release the whole segments into the bowl. Discard any seeds. Set aside.

In a small bowl, combine the vinegar, salt, and pepper to taste. Using a small whisk, stir until the salt dissolves. Add the mustard and honey and whisk until blended. Add the olive oil, a little at a time, and whisk until well blended. Taste and adjust the seasonings. Pour about half of the vinaigrette into a medium bowl.

Using a sharp knife, peel the celery root and shred on the medium holes of a hand-held shredder. Immediately place in the medium bowl holding the mustard vinaigrette. Mix well. (This step can be done up to 1 hour in advance of serving.)

Rinse the lettuces carefully and dry well. If necessary, tear into bite-sized pieces. Place in a large salad bowl. Add the remaining mustard vinaigrette and toss until well mixed.

Divide the lettuces among 6 salad plates, arranging them in a ring on each. Divide the shredded celery root among the plates, placing it in the center. Arrange the orange segments on the lettuces and serve at once.

Serves 6

Roast Pork Loin and Onions

olive oil

1½ lb (750 g) small boiling onions, about
   1 inch (2.5 cm) in diameter (about 30)

1 center-cut boneless pork loin, 2½–3 lb
   (1.25–1.5 kg), trimmed of most fat and
   tied in several places

2 teaspoons chopped fresh thyme, plus
   6 thyme sprigs

salt and freshly ground pepper

½ cup (4 fl oz/125 ml) dry white wine,
   plus extra wine for basting

1 teaspoon cornstarch (cornflour) mixed
   with 1 tablespoon water

*P*osition a rack in the lower third of an oven and preheat to 425°F (220°C). Lightly coat a heavy roasting pan with olive oil.

Trim the onions, then peel and cut a shallow cross in the root end. Fill a saucepan three-fourths full with water and bring to a boil over medium-high heat. Add the onions, return the water to a boil and boil for 2 minutes. Drain the onions and set aside.

Wipe any moisture from the pork loin with paper towels. Rub the loin all over with olive oil. Sprinkle with the chopped thyme and season lightly with salt and pepper. Place the pork loin, fat side up, in the roasting pan (without a rack) and add the ½ cup (4 fl oz/125 ml) wine. Surround the meat with the onions.

Roast, stirring the onions occasionally and basting the meat and onions a few times with the extra wine or the pan juices, until the loin and onions are lightly golden and the juices run clear when the loin is pierced with a knife, 50–70 minutes. To test for doneness, insert an instant-read thermometer into the center of the meat; it should read 160°–165°F (71°–74°C).

Remove from the oven and transfer the roast to a warmed platter; cover loosely with aluminum foil and set aside in a warm place. Using a slotted spoon, transfer the onions to a bowl and cover to keep warm. Pour the juices from the pan into a medium saucepan. Let stand for a few minutes to allow the fat to rise to the surface, then skim off the fat with a large spoon and discard. Stir the cornstarch mixture into the juices, place over medium-low heat and bring to a boil, stirring constantly. When the mixture thickens, season to taste with salt and pepper. If it thickens too much, add a little water or wine to thin to the proper consistency. Return the onions to the sauce and coat well.

To serve, cut the meat into slices ½ inch (12 mm) thick and layer them on the platter. Surround the meat with the onions and their sauce. Garnish with the thyme sprigs.

Serves 6

Brown Rice Pilaf with Pecans

2 tablespoons unsalted butter

1 yellow onion, diced (about 1 cup/
   4 oz/125 g)

1 celery stalk, diced (about ½ cup/
   2½ oz/75 g)

1½ cups (10½ oz/330 g) long-grain
   brown rice

1 teaspoon ground cumin

1 lemon

3 cups (24 fl oz/750 ml) chicken stock

½ teaspoon salt

freshly ground pepper

1½ cups (6 oz/185 g) pecan pieces,
   toasted (*see glossary, page 106*)

2 tablespoons chopped fresh parsley

A welcome change from mashed potatoes, this dish is an exceptional accompaniment to roast pork. It can be prepared up to the point where the pecans are added to the cooked rice, then kept warm over a pan of hot water for up to 1 hour. When ready to serve, heat over very low heat if necessary, then mix in the pecans.

✦

*I*n a large sauté pan or large saucepan over medium-low heat, melt the butter. Add the onion and sauté, stirring occasionally, until translucent, 5–6 minutes. Add the celery, rice and cumin, raise the heat to medium and continue to sauté, stirring, until the onion and celery are tender and the rice is golden, 3–4 minutes. Remove from the heat.

Using a zester or a small shredder and holding the lemon over the pan of rice, shred the zest of the lemon (yellow part only) directly onto the rice. Add the chicken stock, salt, and pepper to taste. Return the pan to medium-high heat and bring to a boil. Reduce the heat to low, cover and simmer until all of the liquid has been absorbed and the rice is tender, 45–60 minutes.

Remove the pan from the heat and let stand, tightly covered, for 10 minutes.

To serve, chop the pecans coarsely. Fluff the rice with a fork and gently incorporate the pecans into the rice. Taste and adjust the seasonings. Transfer to a warmed serving dish and sprinkle with the parsley.

Serves 6

Broccoli and Mushrooms with Lemon

1 bunch broccoli, about 1½ lb (750 g)
¾ lb (375 g) small, firm fresh mushrooms
3 tablespoons fresh lemon juice
3 tablespoons unsalted butter
1 cup (8 fl oz/250 ml) heavy (double)
  cream
salt and freshly ground pepper
1 lemon

Remove the florets from the broccoli stems. Cut any large florets into pieces so that all of the florets are the same size. If the central stems are large, using a paring knife, peel off the tough outer layer and then cut in half lengthwise. Cut the halves crosswise into pieces 1 inch (2.5 cm) long and add to the florets. Set aside.

Clean the mushrooms with a soft brush or clean kitchen towel to remove any soil; do not rinse in water. Trim off the stem ends and then cut the caps vertically into slices ¼ inch (6 mm) thick. Place the lemon juice in a large bowl, add the mushroom slices and toss quickly to coat the slices evenly. The lemon juice prevents the mushrooms from turning dark, plus adds the lemon flavor. (This recipe can be prepared up to this point about 1 hour in advance of beginning the cooking.)

In a large sauté pan or large, deep frying pan over medium heat, melt the butter. Add the mushrooms and sauté, stirring and tossing constantly, until the mushrooms begin to release their liquid, 4–5 minutes. Add the cream, raise the heat to medium-high and cook until the cream thickens a little, 5–6 minutes. Season to taste with salt and pepper. Remove from the heat and set aside.

Fill a large saucepan three-fourths full with water and bring to a boil over medium-high heat. Add the broccoli and 1 tablespoon salt. Boil until the broccoli turns bright green and is tender-crisp, 4–5 minutes. Drain well and arrange on a warmed serving plate or in a bowl.

Reheat the mushrooms and cream quickly to serving temperature and spoon over the broccoli. Using a zester or small shredder and holding the lemon over the broccoli, shred the zest of the lemon (yellow part only) directly onto the broccoli and mushrooms. Serve immediately.

Serves 6

Ginger Steamed Pudding

2 cups (10 oz/315 g) all-purpose (plain) flour

1 teaspoon baking soda (bicarbonate of soda)

⅛ teaspoon salt

4 teaspoons ground ginger

¾ cup (6 oz/185 g) unsalted butter, cut into small cubes

1 cup (7 oz/220 g) firmly packed dark brown sugar

4 eggs

6 oz (185 g) crystallized ginger, coarsely chopped and lightly dusted with flour to prevent sticking

1 cup (8 fl oz/250 ml) heavy (double) cream

2–3 tablespoons confectioners' (icing) sugar

1 teaspoon grated orange zest

*B*utter a deep, heatproof 1½-qt (1.5-l) bowl, a metal steamed-pudding mold with a cover (preferably with a tube) or similar mold. Set aside. Place a wire trivet in a large, deep pot and fill about one-fourth full with water. Bring to a boil. Reduce the heat to low but keep hot. Bring a teakettle of water to a boil; keep warm.

Sift together the flour, baking soda, salt and ground ginger. Set aside. In a bowl, combine the butter and brown sugar and, using an electric mixer, beat at medium speed until light and creamy, 3–4 minutes. Add the eggs, one at a time, beating well after each addition. Using a rubber spatula, fold in the flour mixture, one-third at a time, until blended. Stir in the chopped ginger.

To avoid air pockets, carefully spoon the mixture into the pre-pared mold and then tap the mold on the countertop to level it off. The mold should be about two-thirds full, to allow for expansion. Attach the cover or fit a piece of parchment paper or aluminum foil greased with butter over the top (buttered side down) and secure with kitchen string. Place the mold atop the trivet in the pot. The water should reach about halfway up the sides of the mold; add more boiling water as needed. Bring the water in the pot back to a low boil, reduce the heat, cover the pot and simmer gently for 2 hours if using a heatproof bowl, or 1½ hours if using a metal mold. To test for doneness, insert a toothpick into the center of the pudding; it should come out clean. Transfer from the pot to a rack. Uncover and let stand for 10–15 minutes.

Meanwhile, in a bowl, using a whisk, beat the cream until it begins to thicken. Add the confectioners' sugar to taste and the orange zest. Continue whisking until soft folds form that hold their shape. Do not beat until stiff.

Invert the pudding onto a serving plate. Slice the warm pudding into wedges and transfer to plates. Top with the whipped cream and serve.

Serves 6–8

New Year's Eve Dinner

**BELGIAN ENDIVE SPEARS
WITH CAVIAR AND SOUR CREAM**

MIXED GREENS WITH BEETS AND CUCUMBERS

ROAST RACK OF LAMB WITH HERBED CRUST

POTATO-MUSHROOM GRATIN

SAUTÉ OF JULIENNED GARDEN VEGETABLES

CHOCOLATE BROWNIE PUDDING CAKES

SERVES 6

T HE FINAL EVENING OF THE YEAR CALLS FOR A COMBINATION OF ELEGANCE AND EASE. OUR MENU DELIVERS ELEGANCE IN THE FORM OF INDULGENT INGREDIENTS LIKE CAVIAR, RACK OF LAMB, WILD MUSHROOMS AND CHOCOLATE— PLUS, OF COURSE, FINE CHAMPAGNE. YET, THE RECIPES—LISTED AT THE TABLE ON HANDSOME LITTLE MENU CARDS—ARE PRE- PARED AND PRESENTED WITH SUCH SIMPLICITY THAT YOU CAN JOIN YOUR GUESTS FULLY IN THE CELEBRATION. WE CHOSE ALABASTER DISHES TO SHOW OFF THE MENU AT ITS SPARKLING BEST; YOU CAN SUBSTITUTE YOUR OWN FINEST CHINA OR SILVER SERVING PIECES, OR ANY TABLEWARE THAT COMPLEMENTS THE FOOD. STYLISHLY WRAPPED SMALL GIFTS WELCOME EACH GUEST TO THE TABLE. WE ALSO ADDED A HEALTHY DOSE OF IRREVERENT FUN BY TURNING POCKET-SIZED NOTEPADS INTO PLACE CARDS, READY FOR EACH GUEST TO RECORD HIS OR HER OWN NEW YEAR'S RESOLUTIONS.

❖ Drink Suggestions ❖

Begin with Champagne or sparkling wine. With the lamb, pour a vintage red such as a Cabernet Sauvignon or a Merlot.

❖ Preparation Strategies ❖

Up to 8 hours ahead: prepare the salad ingredients and refrigerate separately.

Up to 6 hours ahead: separate and chill the Belgian endive leaves.

Up to 4 hours ahead: assemble the gratin, parboil the vegetables and sauté the onion, leaving everything at room temperature.

Up to 3 hours ahead: prepare the cake batter, fill the ramekins, cover and leave at room temperature.

Up to 2 hours ahead: prepare the lamb crust mixture.

✦ New Year's Resolution Notepads ✦

The place cards for this New Year's Eve dinner come in the form of notepads in which each guest can record his or her resolutions for the coming year—a great way to break the ice and spark lively conversation. At your local stationer's or variety store, buy small spiral-bound notepads with blank covers, festive gift tags (with strings) about the size of the pads, small bridge or golf pencils, gift wrapping paper, a metallic felt-tip pen and glue. Glue a gift tag to the cover of each pad. Wrap each pencil in a small piece of paper, securing it with glue. Tie a pencil to each gift tag. Using the pen, write guests' names on the pads.

A great icebreaker: New Year's resolution pads.

A triple wrapping for decorative party favors.

✦ Surprise Gifts ✦

As an added decoration for the holiday table, prepare small, inexpensive gifts to leave at each place setting. Here, the gifts are enclosed in little cardboard boxes that are then wrapped in metallic paper, further wrapped in tulle (available at a reasonable cost in fabric stores) and finally tied with a variety of ribbons to complement the table's color scheme. Have guests wait to open their favors after the midnight toast.

75

Belgian Endive Spears with Caviar and Sour Cream

2 large heads Belgian endive (chicory/
witloof)

½ cup (4 fl oz/125 ml) sour cream or
crème fraîche

2 oz (60 g) caviar, salmon roe or golden
caviar, or a combination

2 tablespoons finely chopped fresh chives

This simple first course is both festive and light. For the freshest flavor and the most attractive presentation, fill the leaves just before serving.

✤✦

Remove the outer leaves of the endives and reserve them for the mixed green salad (page 78). Then separate from the heart the tenderest leaves that are large enough for filling. Again, reserve the smallest leaves for the salad. There should be 6–8 leaves from each endive that can be used for filling. Place them in a plastic bag and chill in the refrigerator for up to 6 hours before continuing.

At serving time, spoon a dollop of sour cream or crème fraîche onto the pointed end of each endive leaf. Then, using a ½ teaspoon measure, garnish the sour cream with the caviar. Sprinkle lightly with the chives, arrange on a platter and serve immediately.

Serves 6

Mixed Greens with Beets and Cucumbers

2 beets

FOR THE DRESSING:
1 shallot, finely chopped
1 tablespoon whole-grain mustard
2 tablespoons fresh lemon juice
2 tablespoons balsamic vinegar
¾ cup (6 fl oz/180 ml) olive oil
½ teaspoon salt
¼ teaspoon freshly ground pepper
2 tablespoons finely chopped fresh
   parsley

2 heads butter (Boston) lettuce, cored,
   leaves separated and torn into bite-sized
   pieces
1 small head radicchio (red chicory),
   cored, leaves separated and torn into
   bite-sized pieces
2 heads Belgian endive (chicory/witloof),
   thinly sliced (you can include the
   remaining leaves from the recipe on
   page 77)
1 cucumber, peeled, halved lengthwise,
   seeded and cut into slices ½ inch
   (12 mm) thick
⅓ cup (1½ oz/45 g) walnuts, coarsely
   chopped and toasted (*see glossary,*
   page 106)

The toasted walnuts and rosy chopped beets contribute plenty of texture to this pretty salad. Sliced cucumber adds another crunch. The dressing is nicely balanced, combining rich balsamic and light lemon flavors with pungent shallots and grainy mustard.

⊁⊰

*F*ill a saucepan three-fourths full with water and bring to a boil. Meanwhile, trim off all but ½ inch (12 mm) of each beet stem. Do not cut off the root ends. Immerse the beets in the boiling water and cook until tender but still slightly resistant when pierced, 25–35 minutes, depending upon their size.

To make the dressing, in a bowl, combine the shallot, mustard, lemon juice and vinegar and whisk to mix. Slowly add the oil, whisking constantly until completely blended. Whisk in the salt, pepper and parsley. Taste and adjust the seasonings. Set aside.

Drain the beets and, when cool enough to handle, trim off the stems and roots. Peel the beets, then finely chop them and set aside. Ready the lettuce, radicchio, endive and cucumber. (The salad can be prepared up to this point 8 hours in advance. Cover and refrigerate the dressing, beets, greens and cucumber separately; bring the dressing to room temperature before using.)

In a large bowl, combine the lettuce, radicchio and endive. Drizzle half of the dressing over the greens and toss to coat evenly. Divide the greens evenly among 6 salad plates and decorate each serving with the beets and cucumbers. Strew the toasted walnuts over the top. Serve the remaining dressing in a bowl on the side.

Serves 6

Roast Rack of Lamb with Herbed Crust

2 racks of lamb, 8 chops or about 2½ lb
  (1.25 kg) each
1 cup (2 oz/60 g) fresh French bread
  crumbs
2 shallots, finely chopped
1 tablespoon finely chopped fresh basil
1 tablespoon finely chopped fresh thyme,
  plus thyme sprigs for garnish
2 tablespoons finely chopped fresh
  parsley
¼ teaspoon salt
⅛ teaspoon freshly ground pepper
3 tablespoons olive oil
2 tablespoons chicken stock

This variation on parslied rack of lamb uses a Provençal-style mixture of herbs. Don't worry if the coating falls off when you carve the lamb; simply press it back in place when you arrange the lamb chops on the plate. For a nice presentation, crisscross the ends of the lamb chops.

>‹

Preheat an oven to 450°F (230°C). Trim any excess fat from the lamb racks. Using a small, sharp knife, scrape off any meat from the top 1½ inches (4 cm) of each bone.

Place the lamb racks in a roasting pan, bone side down, and roast for 18–25 minutes for medium-rare. The timing will depend upon their size. To test for doneness, insert an instant-read meat thermometer into the thickest part of the lamb away from the bone; it should register 135°F (57°C).

While the meat is roasting, in a small bowl, combine the bread crumbs, shallots, basil, chopped thyme, parsley, salt, pepper, olive oil and chicken stock and mix well. (You can prepare this mixture up to 2 hours in advance of when the meat is ready; set aside at room temperature.)

Preheat the broiler (griller). When the lamb racks are done roasting, spread the bread crumb mixture evenly over the meat side of the racks. Place the lamb under the broiler about 3 inches (7.5 cm) from the heat source and broil (grill) until lightly browned, 2–3 minutes. Be careful the coating does not burn.

Transfer the racks to a serving platter. Separate the chops by cutting between the bones. Serve 2 or 3 chops per person, garnishing the plates with thyme. Serve immediately.

Serves 6

Potato-Mushroom Gratin

1 tablespoon unsalted butter

1 tablespoon olive oil, plus extra for dish

1½ lb (750 g) mixed fresh wild mushrooms such as chanterelles, porcini and morels, brushed clean and thinly sliced

1 clove garlic, minced

2½ lb (1.25 kg) waxy, white-fleshed potatoes

1¼ cups (10 fl oz/310 ml) milk

1 cup (8 fl oz/250 ml) heavy (double) cream

1 teaspoon salt

⅛ teaspoon freshly ground pepper

1 cup (4 oz/125 g) shredded Gruyère cheese

3 tablespoons fine dried bread crumbs

In a large frying pan over medium heat, melt the butter with the olive oil. Add the mushrooms and sauté until softened, 5–7 minutes. Add the garlic and sauté for 1 minute longer. Remove from the heat and set aside.

Peel the potatoes, then cut them into uniform slices no more than ⅛ inch (3 mm) thick (a food processor fitted with the fine slicing disk works well for this step). Place the slices in a kitchen towel and wring tightly with your hands to remove excess moisture. Pour the milk into a large, deep, heavy-bottomed saucepan over medium-high heat. Add the potatoes, separating the pieces as you drop them into the pan, and bring to a boil. Cover, reduce the heat to low and simmer for 10 minutes. Stir with a wooden spoon occasionally to prevent the potatoes from sticking. Remove the cover and continue to simmer until most of the milk has been absorbed, about 3 minutes more.

Add the cream, salt and pepper and again bring to a boil. Reduce the heat to low, cover and simmer until there is still some liquid left but the potatoes are very soft, about 10 minutes; stir with a wooden spoon occasionally to prevent sticking. Remove the cover and continue to simmer until almost all of the cream has been absorbed, about 3 minutes more. Season with salt and pepper to taste. Remove from the heat.

Oil a 9-inch (23-cm) flameproof baking dish with 2-inch (5-cm) sides. Transfer half of the potato mixture to the dish and top with the mushrooms. Cover with the remaining potatoes. Sprinkle with the cheese and then the crumbs. (The dish can be prepared up to this point 4 hours in advance and kept at room temperature.)

Preheat a broiler (griller). Place the dish about 4 inches (10 cm) from the heat source and broil (grill) until nicely browned on top, 8–10 minutes. Watch carefully, as the topping will burn easily. Serve immediately.

Serves 6

Sauté of Julienned Garden Vegetables

4 medium carrots
4 medium celery stalks
¾ lb (375 g) young, slender green beans
   such as haricots verts
1 tablespoon unsalted butter
1 tablespoon olive oil
1 red (Spanish) onion, thinly sliced
½ teaspoon salt
pinch of cracked pepper
1 tablespoon finely chopped fresh parsley

Colorful and garden fresh, these mixed vegetables will add sparkle to your holiday main-course plate.

✈

Peel the carrots. Trim away the tough ends and any strings from the celery stalks. Cut the carrots and celery stalks into 2-by-¼-by-¼-inch (5-cm-by-6-mm-by-6-mm) julienne strips; keep them separate. Trim off the stem ends from the green beans and, if the beans are large and more than 2 inches (5 cm) long, cut them into julienne strips to match the carrots and celery.

Fill a saucepan three-fourths full with water and bring to a boil. Immerse the carrots in the water and boil for 1 minute. Using a slotted spoon, scoop out the carrots, draining well, and set aside. Immerse the celery in the same boiling water and boil for 30 seconds, then scoop them out and set aside. Finally, immerse the green beans in the boiling water and boil for 2 minutes; drain well and set aside.

In a frying pan over medium heat, melt the butter with the olive oil. Add the onion and sauté, stirring, until soft and slightly browned, 3–5 minutes. (The recipe can be prepared up to this point and set aside for 4 hours at room temperature before continuing.) Add the carrots, celery and green beans and continue to sauté until the vegetables are tender but not too soft, about 3 minutes longer. Add the salt, pepper and parsley and mix well. Taste and adjust the seasonings.

Transfer to a serving dish and serve immediately.

Serves 6

Chocolate Brownie Pudding Cakes

5½ oz (170 g) good-quality bittersweet chocolate, cut into small pieces

½ cup (4 oz/125 g) plus 1 tablespoon unsalted butter

3 whole eggs, plus 3 egg yolks

⅓ cup (3 oz/90 g) granulated sugar

5 tablespoons (1½ oz/45 g) all-purpose (plain) flour

confectioners' (icing) sugar for dusting

whipped cream for serving, optional

Although rich and chocolatey, this dessert is not overly heavy. It is particularly well suited to a New Year's Eve menu, because it can be assembled completely in advance and then popped into the oven to bake just before serving.

⇥⇤

Preheat an oven to 375°F (190°C). Lightly butter six 1-cup (8-fl oz/ 250-ml) ramekins and set aside.

Place the chocolate and butter in a heatproof bowl or the top pan of a double boiler. Set over a pan of gently simmering water but not touching the water. Stir with a wooden spoon until the chocolate is melted and smooth. Remove from the pan of water and let cool completely.

Place the whole eggs, egg yolks and granulated sugar in a bowl and, using an electric mixer set on medium speed, beat until a light lemon color, about 5 minutes. Add the flour and continue to beat on medium speed until fully blended. Then add the cooled chocolate-butter mixture and beat again until blended. Divide the batter among the prepared ramekins, filling each halfway. (The recipe can be prepared up to this point, lightly covered with aluminum foil or plastic wrap and set aside at room temperature for up to 3 hours before baking.)

Set the ramekins on a baking sheet and place in the oven. Bake until the cakes are set but the centers still move slightly when the ramekins are shaken, about 10½ minutes. Do not overbake or the cakes will be dry instead of creamy in the center. Remove from the oven and, using a sieve, dust the tops with confectioners' sugar.

Place the ramekins on dessert plates and place a dollop of whipped cream on each cake, if desired. Serve immediately.

Serves 6

New Year's Day Buffet

———◆———

FILO PIZZA WITH FETA, SUN-DRIED
TOMATOES AND OLIVES

BLACK AND WHITE BEAN SALAD WITH FENNEL
AND RED PEPPER

GARDEN SALAD WITH PEARS, PECANS
AND GORGONZOLA

COUSCOUS WITH CHICKEN, CHICK-PEAS AND
WINTER VEGETABLES

WARM LEMON RICE CUSTARDS

SPICY GINGER BARS

SERVES 12

✣ BUNDLING NAPKINS & FLATWARE ✦
For a neater buffet presentation, and to help guests serve themselves more easily, prepare individual bundles consisting of a napkin and flatware. Neatly fold each napkin into a rectangle and place a fork and knife on top. Crisscross a pretty ribbon over the cutlery and around the napkin, tying it at the back. Arrange the bundles on the buffet table next to the plates.

Napkin and flatware, wrapped as prettily as a present.

No holiday calls for more fuss-free entertaining than New Year's Day. That is why we put together a menu of uncomplicated dishes that you can prepare for the most part a day ahead of time or at least several hours before people arrive. To make the party even more relaxed, the menu is designed to be served buffet style so that everyone can help themselves at their own leisurely pace. To highlight the spirit of casual comfort, we chose to present the menu on a coffee table beside the fireplace, surrounded by brightly colored flower arrangements that emphasize the gathering's informal spirit. Be sure to have plenty of seating around the room, loosely grouped to encourage conversation. Individual bundles of cutlery (left) should include oversized napkins large enough to completely cover guests' laps while they eat.

✤ DRINK SUGGESTIONS ✥

Many guests will want nonalcoholic drinks the day after a night of revelry. Iced ginger mint tea goes well with this menu; you can find it in well-stocked markets, or make it yourself by brewing mint tea with slices of fresh ginger. Offer bottled waters, too, and white wine and beer for those who'd like them.

✤ PREPARATION STRATEGIES ✥

Up to 2 days ahead: make the ginger bars.

Up to 1 day ahead: assemble the filo pizza; cook and drain the beans; rinse and refrigerate the salad greens; prepare the rice custards and refrigerate.

Several hours ahead: cook the chick-peas and chicken for the couscous; cook the rice custards, if you wish to serve them at room temperature.

✤ FLOWER-AND-FRUIT ARRANGEMENTS ✥

Florists and amateur flower arrangers often use pebbles or other objects to anchor flowers in vases. Here, fruits are used to create arrangements that add a bright, fresh look to the holiday table. Start with glass vases large enough to hold several small whole fruits such as the lemons, limes and tangerines shown. Put the fruits in the vases and add cold water. Insert flowers with sturdy stems, wedging the stems securely between the fruits.

Gerbera daisies and fruit add a burst of color to the buffet.

Filo Pizza with Feta, Sun-Dried Tomatoes and Olives

20 sheets filo dough, each about 14 by
   10 inches (35 by 25 cm), thawed in
   the refrigerator if frozen
2 tablespoons unsalted butter
3 tablespoons olive oil
½ lb (250 g) mozzarella cheese, shredded
   (2 cups)
¼ lb (125 g) feta cheese, finely crumbled
   (¾ cup)
½ cup (3 oz/90 g) oil-cured black olives,
   pitted and chopped
½ cup (3 oz/90 g) drained oil-packed
   sun-dried tomatoes, chopped
4 green (spring) onions, including some
   tender green tops, thinly sliced
2 tablespoons chopped fresh mint

This pizza can be fully assembled a day in advance, stored in the refrigerator and baked when needed.

><

*I*f necessary, trim the filo sheets to measure 14 by 10 inches (35 by 25 cm). Immediately cover the filo with a lightly dampened towel to prevent them from drying out.

In a small saucepan over medium-low heat, melt the butter with the olive oil. Remove from the heat; set alongside the work surface.

Place about ¾ cup (3 oz/90 g) of the mozzarella in a bowl. Add the feta, olives, sun-dried tomatoes, green onions and mint and stir to mix well.

Position a rack in the upper third of an oven and preheat to 400°F (200°C).

Using a pastry brush, lightly coat a 12-by-15-inch (30-by-37.5-cm) baking sheet with some of the butter-oil mixture. Place 1 filo sheet on the baking sheet and brush it lightly with the butter-oil mixture. Cover it with a second filo sheet and brush it lightly with the butter-oil mixture. Then sprinkle it evenly with about ¼ cup of the cheese mixture. Continue stacking in the same manner, brushing each filo sheet with the butter-oil mixture and sprinkling each second sheet with some of the filling, until all of the filo and filling have been used. Brush the top layer with the butter-oil mixture. Sprinkle the remaining 1¼ cups (5 oz/160 g) mozzarella cheese evenly over the top.

Bake until the cheese melts and the filo is golden and crisp on the edges, 25–35 minutes. Remove from the oven and immediately slide the filo pizza off the sheet onto a large, decorative cutting board. Cut into 2-inch (5-cm) squares and serve hot or warm directly from the board.

Makes 35; serves 12

Black and White Bean Salad with Fennel and Red Pepper

¾ cup (5½ oz/170 g) dried small white (navy) beans

¾ cup (5½ oz/170 g) dried black beans

½ cup (4 fl oz/125 ml) red wine vinegar

⅔ cup (5 fl oz/160 ml) extra-virgin olive oil

5 cloves garlic, minced

salt and freshly ground pepper

3 fennel bulbs with tops, 1¼–1½ lb (625–750 g) total weight

1 small red (Spanish) onion, cut into ¼-inch (6-mm) dice

8 green (spring) onions, including tender green tops, cut into slices ¼ inch (6 mm) thick

1 large red bell pepper (capsicum), seeded, deribbed and cut into ¼-inch (6-mm) dice

⅓ cup (½ oz/15 g) chopped fresh parsley

The variety of ingredients in this salad adds color to any buffet table. If you prefer, use all white or all black beans. Place the salad in a large serving bowl and garnish with big, leafy sprigs of Italian parsley.

✦

Pick over the white beans and discard any damaged beans or stones. Rinse the beans in water and place in a bowl. Add water to cover generously and let soak for 3 hours. Do the same steps with the black beans, putting them in a separate bowl.

Drain the beans and place them in separate saucepans. Add water to cover by 2 inches (5 cm) to each pan and bring to a boil over high heat. Reduce the heat to low and simmer, uncovered, until the beans are tender. The white beans will take 35–45 minutes and the black beans will take 45–60 minutes. Drain the beans and set them aside. (The beans can be cooked up to 1 day in advance, then drained, covered and refrigerated.)

In a large bowl, whisk together the vinegar, olive oil, garlic, and salt and pepper to taste. Add the black and white beans and toss to mix well. Cover and refrigerate until completely cool, about 1 hour.

Meanwhile, trim off the tops from the fennel bulbs and reserve. Cut away the cores and bruised areas on the bulbs and then cut the bulbs into ¼-inch (6-mm) dice. Chop the reserved tops. Add the chopped fennel tops and diced fennel, red onion, green onions, bell pepper and parsley to the beans and toss to mix well. Season to taste with salt and pepper and serve at room temperature.

Serves 12

Garden Salad with Pears, Pecans and Gorgonzola

¾ lb (375 g) loosely packed mixed
  salad greens
3 tablespoons sherry vinegar
2 tablespoons red wine vinegar
2 tablespoons walnut or other flavorful
  nut oil, optional
¾ cup (6 fl oz/180 ml) extra-virgin olive
  oil
salt and freshly ground pepper
⅔ cup (2½ oz/75 g) pecan halves, toasted
  (see glossary, page 106)
3 slightly firm pears such as Bosc or
  Comice, halved, cored and thinly sliced
  lengthwise
½ lb (250 g) Gorgonzola cheese

This is a perfect salad for winter. Pears are in season, and the flavors of the fruit, pecans and Gorgonzola are wonderfully complementary. Make sure that you don't toss the salad with the dressing too early or the greens will wilt; toss just before serving. Walnuts and goat cheese can be used in place of the pecans and Gorgonzola.

✜

*R*inse the salad greens carefully to remove any dirt or grit and dry well. Place the greens in a plastic bag or in a salad bowl with a damp kitchen towel over the top and place in the refrigerator to crisp for up to 24 hours.

In a small bowl, whisk together the sherry vinegar, red wine vinegar, nut oil (if using) and olive oil until well blended. Season to taste with salt and pepper.

Place the greens in a large salad bowl. Add the pecans, pears and dressing and toss well. Taste and adjust the seasonings. Crumble the cheese on top and serve immediately.

Serves 12

Couscous with Chicken, Chick-peas and Winter Vegetables

1 cup (7 oz/220 g) dried chick-peas (garbanzo beans)

2 tablespoons unsalted butter

6 lb (3 kg) assorted chicken pieces such as breasts, drumsticks and thighs, skin and any visible fat removed

2 teaspoons salt

1 teaspoon freshly ground pepper

½ teaspoon powdered saffron

2 teaspoons ground turmeric

1 tablespoon ground cumin

4 yellow onions, quartered

8 cloves garlic, chopped

4 cinnamon sticks, each about 3 inches (7.5 cm) long

2½ qt (2.5 l) plus 5 cups (40 fl oz/1.25 l) water

1½ lb (750 g) carrots, peeled and cut into 1-inch (2.5-cm) lengths

1½ lb (750 g) small turnips, peeled and cut through the stem end into eighths

4 cups (1¼ lb/625 g) couscous

3½ cups (7 oz/220 g) broccoli florets

1 fresh jalapeño chili pepper, halved

½ cup (¾ oz/20 g) chopped fresh cilantro (fresh coriander)

Pick over the chick-peas and discard any damaged peas or stones. Rinse and place in a bowl. Add water to cover generously and let soak for about 3 hours.

Drain the chick-peas and place in a saucepan. Add water to cover by 2 inches (5 cm) and bring to a boil. Reduce the heat to low and simmer, uncovered, until tender, 50–60 minutes. Drain and set aside.

In a 6-qt (6-l) soup pot over medium-high heat, melt the butter. Add the chicken pieces, 1 teaspoon of the salt, the pepper, saffron, turmeric, cumin, onions, garlic and cinnamon sticks. Stir to mix well, cover and cook until the chicken just begins to turn white, about 15 minutes. Add the chick-peas and the 2½ qt (2.5 l) water; raise the heat to high and bring to a boil. Reduce the heat to medium-low, cover and simmer until the chicken is opaque throughout when pierced, about 20 minutes. Add the carrots and turnips and continue to simmer, covered, until the vegetables are tender and the chicken meat is almost falling from the bones, about 20 minutes longer. (The recipe can be prepared up to this point several hours in advance; let cool, cover and refrigerate.)

Fifteen minutes before serving, in a saucepan, bring the 5 cups (40 fl oz/1.25 l) water to a boil. Add the remaining 1 teaspoon salt and the couscous and stir to mix well. Remove from the heat, cover and let stand for 15 minutes or according to package directions.

Meanwhile, bring the chicken mixture to a boil. Add the broccoli and jalapeño, cover and simmer over medium heat until the broccoli is tender, about 10 minutes. Adjust the seasonings.

To serve, spoon the couscous onto a platter, making a well in the center. Using a slotted spoon, place the chicken and vegetables in the well; discard the jalapeño and cinnamon. Moisten the couscous with about one-fourth of the broth. Sprinkle the cilantro over all. Serve the remaining broth on the side.

Serves 12

Warm Lemon Rice Custards

3 tablespoons unsalted butter

1 cup (7 oz/220 g) short-grain white rice

3 cups (24 fl oz/750 ml) milk

1 tablespoon grated lemon zest

¾ cup (6 oz/185 g) granulated sugar

3 whole eggs, plus 3 egg yolks

1 tablespoon fresh lemon juice

boiling water, as needed

confectioners' (icing) sugar for dusting

These custards can be served warm, or you can bake them several hours in advance and serve at room temperature. Let the custards cool completely, cover and store in the refrigerator, then remove from the refrigerator about 20 minutes before serving.

✦✦

Preheat an oven to 400°F (200°C). Using 1 tablespoon of the butter, grease twelve 5-fl oz (160-ml) ramekins.

Fill a 2-qt (2-l) saucepan three-fourths full with water and bring to a boil. Add the rice, bring just to a boil, reduce the heat to medium and simmer for 5 minutes. Drain and set aside.

Pour the milk into the same saucepan and bring to a boil over medium heat. Add the rice and lemon zest. Cook, stirring occasionally, until the rice is tender and the milk is absorbed, about 20 minutes. Remove from the heat; add the granulated sugar and the remaining 2 tablespoons butter. Stir until dissolved.

In a large bowl, whisk together the whole eggs, egg yolks and lemon juice until blended. Add one-fourth of the hot rice to the eggs and stir together. Continue to add the rice slowly, stirring constantly, until all of the rice has been added; do not add the hot rice to the eggs too quickly or the eggs will scramble. Spoon the mixture into the prepared ramekins, dividing it evenly. (The custards can be prepared up to this point 1 day in advance, covered and refrigerated. Twenty minutes before you are ready to bake them, remove from the refrigerator.)

Set the ramekins in a baking pan and pour boiling water into the pan to reach halfway up the sides of the dishes. Cover the pan with aluminum foil and bake until a skewer inserted into the center of a custard comes out clean, 30–35 minutes. Remove from the oven and let cool for 10–20 minutes. Using a sieve, dust the tops with confectioners' sugar and serve.

Serves 12

Spicy Ginger Bars

¾ cup (6 oz/185 g) unsalted butter, at
   room temperature
¾ cup (5½ oz/170 g) firmly packed dark
   brown sugar
½ cup (4 oz/125 g) granulated sugar
2 eggs
1 tablespoon molasses
2¼ cups (11½ oz/360 g) all-purpose
   (plain) flour
¼ teaspoon salt
1 teaspoon baking soda (bicarbonate
   of soda)
1½ teaspoons ground ginger
½ teaspoon ground cloves
½ cup (2½ oz/75 g) crystallized ginger,
   cut into ¼-inch (6-mm) dice

*Ginger lovers, beware! These soft and chewy bars are addictive. For
a delicious variation, fold in a rounded ¾ cup (5 oz/155 g) semisweet
chocolate chips with the crystallized ginger. The bars can be made
2 days in advance, covered with aluminum foil and stored at room
temperature. Or freeze them for up to 1 month.*

✦

Preheat an oven to 375°F (190°C). Grease a 9-by-13-inch (23-by-
33-cm) baking pan with butter. Dust with flour, tapping out the
excess.

   In a bowl, using an electric mixer set on medium speed, beat
together the butter, brown sugar and granulated sugar until light,
creamy and smooth, 3–4 minutes. Add the eggs, one at a time,
beating thoroughly after each addition until creamy. Beat in the
molasses.

   In a separate bowl, sift together the flour, salt, baking soda,
ground ginger and cloves. Add the flour mixture to the butter
mixture and beat well on low speed until thoroughly combined.
Add the crystallized ginger and stir to mix well. Pour the batter
into the prepared pan.

   Bake until the top is golden, about 30 minutes. Remove from
the oven and let cool completely in the pan on a rack. Cut into
48 bars, each about 1½ inches (4 cm) square.

Makes 4 dozen; serves 12

Glossary

The following glossary defines terms specifically as they relate to holiday menus, including major and unusual ingredients and basic techniques.

ALLSPICE
Sweet spice of Caribbean origin with a flavor suggesting a blend of cinnamon, cloves and nutmeg, hence its name. May be purchased as whole dried berries or ground. Just before using whole berries, bruise them—gently crush them with the bottom of a pan or other heavy instrument—to release more of their flavor.

APPLES
Primarily a late-summer to autumn crop, apples are a favorite fruit of the holiday season. There are literally thousands of apple varieties, so the home cook may sometimes be bewildered when a recipe calls for an apple by specific name or by general type. Tart green apples, often used in cooking, include Granny Smiths, Newtown Pippins and Bramleys. Among the large, sweet varieties are Romes, Baldwins and McIntoshes. Lady apples, sweet and tart in flavor, are prized for their red-tinged yellow skins and their small size, no more than 1–2 inches (2.5–5 cm) in diameter.

To core an apple: Using a small, sharp knife, cut the apple into quarters through the stem and flower ends. Then, cut out the seeds and fibrous core section from each quarter. Alternatively, using an apple corer, press its sharp edges firmly down through the stem end to cut out the core whole.

CARDAMOM
Sweet, exotic-tasting spice mainly used in Middle Eastern and Indian cooking and in Scandinavian baking. Its small, round seeds, which come enclosed inside a husklike pod, are best purchased whole, then ground with a spice grinder or with a mortar and pestle as needed.

CAVIARS & ROES
All manner of fish eggs, or roes, are preserved with salt, which highlights their subtle, briny flavor. The term *caviar* is traditionally reserved for sturgeon roe, which is the finest of the roes. Other commonly available varieties are carp, salmon and whitefish roes. Eaten as special-occasion hors d'oeuvres in their own right, caviars and other roes can also be used as garnishes. A good selection may be found in some specialty-food stores and delicatessens.

CELERY ROOT
Large, knobby root of a species of celery plant, with a crisp texture and fine flavor closely resembling the familiar stalks. Choose smaller, younger roots, to be peeled and eaten raw or cooked. Also known as celeriac.

COUSCOUS
North African staple, also popular in France, these small, granular particles of semolina pasta develop a fluffy consistency resembling rice pilaf when cooked. Served as an accompaniment to stews, braises or other foods with sauces, or used as the base for salads.

CRANBERRIES
Round, deep red, tart berries, grown primarily in wet, sandy bogs in the northeastern United States. Available fresh during the late autumn and frozen year-round.

CREAM, HEAVY
Whipping cream with a butterfat content of at least 36 percent. For the best flavor and cooking properties, purchase 100 percent natural fresh cream with a short shelf life printed on the carton; avoid long-lasting varieties that have been processed by ultraheat methods. In Britain, use double cream.

CHEESES
In its many forms, cheese makes an excellent ingredient in or garnish for holiday meals. For the best selection and finest quality, buy cheese from a well-stocked food store or delicatessen that offers a wide variety and has a frequent turnover of product. The commonly available cheeses called for in this book include:

Blue
Blue-veined cheeses of many varieties have rich, tangy flavors and creamy to crumbly consistencies. Among them are Roquefort, a French cheese made from sheep's milk, with a creamy consistency and a rich, sharp taste; Gorgonzola (below), a semisoft Italian variety; and Maytag blue, an American product that is generally milder than its European counterparts and with a fairly firm consistency.

Cream Cheese
Smooth, white, mild-tasting cheese made from cream and milk, used on its own as a spread or as an ingredient that adds rich flavor and texture to cooked dishes.

Feta
White, salty, sharp-tasting cheese made from sheep's or goat's milk, with a crumbly, creamy-to-dry consistency.

Gruyère
Variety of Swiss cheese with a firm, smooth texture, small holes and a relatively strong flavor.

Mozzarella
Rindless white, mild-tasting Italian cheese traditionally made from water buffalo's milk and sold fresh. Commercially produced and packaged cow's milk mozzarella is now much more common, although it has less flavor. Look for fresh mozzarella sold immersed in water.

Parmesan
Hard, thick-crusted Italian cow's milk cheese with a sharp, salty, full flavor resulting from at least 2 years of aging. The finest Italian variety is designated Parmigiano-Reggiano.® Buy in block form, to grate fresh as needed.

To whip heavy cream, first chill it well in the refrigerator to solidify its butterfat content partially and thus help it to thicken. Pour it into a chilled bowl. Using a wire whisk or a hand-held electric beater set on slow speed, beat until the cream begins to look foamy; then beat more quickly in a circular motion. When the whisk or beaters leave faint traces on the cream's surface, it is lightly whipped; stiffly whipped cream will hold a peak when the whisk or beaters are lifted out. Do not beat further or the cream will become butter.

CRÈME FRAÎCHE

French-style lightly soured and thickened fresh cream. Increasingly available in food markets, although a similar product may be prepared at home by stirring 2 teaspoons well-drained sour cream into 1 cup (8 fl oz/250 ml) lightly whipped heavy (double) cream. Or, to make your own crème fraîche,

stir 1 teaspoon cultured butter-milk into 1 cup (8 fl oz/250 ml) heavy cream. Cover tightly and leave at warm room temperature until thickened, about 12 hours. Refrigerate until ready to serve. Will keep for up to 1 week.

CUMIN

Middle Eastern spice with a strong, dusky, aromatic flavor, popular in cuisines of its region of origin along with those of Latin America, India and parts of Europe. Sold either ground or as whole, small crescent-shaped seeds.

FENNEL

Crisp, refreshing, mildly anise-flavored bulb vegetable, sometimes called by its Italian name, *finocchio*. Another related variety of the bulb is valued for its fine, feathery leaves and stems, which are used as a fresh or dried herb, and for its small, crescent-shaped seeds, dried and used as a spice.

FILO

Tissue-thin sheets of flour-and-water pastry used throughout the Middle East as crisp wrappers for savory or sweet fillings. Usually found in the frozen-food section of well-stocked food stores, or purchased fresh in Middle Eastern delicatessens; defrost frozen filo thoroughly in the refrigerator before use. The fragile sheets, which generally measure about 10 by 14 inches (25 by 35 cm), must be separated and handled carefully to avoid tearing. As you work with the filo, keep the unused sheets covered with a lightly dampened towel to prevent drying.

FRANGELICO

Italian sweet liqueur based on wild hazelnuts and herbs.

GELATIN, UNFLAVORED

Unflavored commercial gelatin gives delicate body to sweet and savory dishes. Sold in envelopes

holding about 1 tablespoon (¼ oz/7 g), each of which is sufficient to jell about 2 cups (16 fl oz/500 ml) liquid.

HALF-AND-HALF

A commercial dairy product consisting of half milk and half light cream. In Britain it is known as half cream.

MARSALA

Dry or sweet amber Italian wine from the area of Marsala, in Sicily.

MOLASSES

Thick, robust-tasting, syrupy sugarcane by-product of sugar refining. Light molasses results from the first boiling of the syrup; dark molasses from the second boiling.

MUSTARDS

Dijon mustard is made in Dijon, France, from dark brown mustard seeds (unless otherwise marked *blanc*) and white wine or wine

---

HERBS

A wide variety of fresh and dried herbs add flavor and variety to festive dishes. Those called for in this book are:

Basil
Sweet, spicy herb popular in Italian and French cooking.

Bay Leaf
Dried whole leaf of the bay laurel tree (below). Pungent and spicy, bay leaves flavor simmered dishes, marinades and pickling mixtures.

Chives
Long, thin green shoots with a mild flavor reminiscent of the onion, to which they are

related. Although chives are available dried in the herb-and-spice section of food stores, fresh chives possess the best flavor.

Cilantro
Green, leafy herb (below) resembling flat-leaf (Italian) parsley, with a sharp, aromatic, somewhat astringent flavor. Popular in Latin American and Asian cuisines. Also called fresh coriander and sometimes Chinese parsley.

Dill
Herb with fine, feathery leaves and sweet, aromatic flavor. Sold fresh and dried.

Mint
Refreshing herb available in many varieties, with spearmint the most common. Used fresh to flavor a broad range of savory and sweet ingredients.

Parsley
This popular fresh herb is sold in two varieties, the readily available curly-leaf type and a flat-leaf type. The latter, also known as Italian parsley, has a more pronounced flavor and is usually preferred.

Rosemary
Mediterranean herb, used either fresh or dried, with an aromatic flavor well suited to lamb and veal, as well as poultry, seafood and vegetables. Strong in flavor, it should be used sparingly, except when grilling.

Sage
Pungent herb, used either fresh or dried, that goes particularly well with fresh or cured pork, lamb, veal or poultry.

Tarragon
Fragrant, distinctively sweet herb (below) used fresh or dried as a seasoning for salads, seafood, chicken, light meats, eggs and vegetables.

Thyme
Clean-tasting, small-leaved herb popular fresh or dried as a seasoning for poultry, light meats, seafood or vegetables.

MUSHROOMS

With their meaty textures and rich, earthy flavors, mushrooms add a touch of luxury to many festive meals. Cultivated white and brown mushrooms are widely available. In their smallest form, with their caps still closed, they are often descriptively called button mushrooms (below).

Chanterelles (below), subtly flavored, usually pale yellow, trumpet-shaped wild mushrooms about 2–3 inches (5–7.5 cm) in length, are also cultivated commercially.

Morels are a flavorful, fairly rare variety with honey-combed conical or globe-shaped caps, enjoyed fresh or dried. Porcini (below), also known by the French term *cèpes,* are popular wild mushrooms with a rich, meaty flavor. Most commonly sold in dried form in Italian delicatessens and specialty-food shops, they are reconstituted in liquid as a flavoring for soups, stews, sauces and stuffings.

vinegar. Pale in color, fairly hot and sharp tasting, true Dijon mustard and non-French blends labeled Dijon style are widely available in food stores. Coarse-grained mustards, sometimes referred to as whole-grain mustards, have a granular texture due to roughly ground mustard seeds; they include the French *moutarde de Meaux* and a number of high-quality British and German varieties.

NUTS

Rich and mellow in flavor, crisp and crunchy in texture, a wide variety of nuts complements both sweet and savory recipes. For the best selection, look in a specialty-food shop, health-food store or the food market baking section.

Toasting brings out the full flavor and aroma of nuts. To toast nuts, preheat an oven to 325°F (165°C). Spread the nuts in a single layer on a baking sheet and place in the oven until they are fragrant and just begin to change color, 5–10 minutes. Remove from the oven and let cool to room temperature. Toasting also loosens the skins of nuts such as hazelnuts and walnuts, which may be removed by wrapping the still-warm nuts in a cotton towel and rubbing against them with the palms of your hands.

OILS

Oils not only provide a medium in which foods may be browned without sticking, but can also subtly enhance the flavor of many dishes. Store oils in airtight containers away from heat and light.

Extra-virgin olive oil, extracted from olives on the first pressing without use of heat or chemicals, is prized for its pure, fruity taste and golden to pale green hue. The higher-priced extra-virgin olive oils are usually of better quality. Products labeled pure olive oil, less aromatic and flavorful, may be used for all-purpose cooking.

Walnut and hazelnut oils are reminiscent of the flavor of the nuts from which they were pressed.

Flavorless vegetable and seed oils such as safflower, canola and corn oil are employed for their high cooking temperatures and bland flavor.

ORANGE, BLOOD

Available in winter months, this variety of orange is notable for its red-blushed orange skin, red pulp and more intense orange flavor. Regular oranges, however, may be substituted.

PAPRIKA

Powdered spice derived from the dried paprika pepper; popular in several European cuisines and available in sweet, mild and hot forms. Hungarian paprika is the best, but Spanish paprika, which is mild, may also be used. Buy in small quantities from shops with a high turnover, to ensure a fresh, flavorful supply.

PEARS

Several pear varieties are available seasonally in markets. Comice pears are large, with short necks and greenish skin highlighted with a red blush. Long, slender, tapered Bosc pears (below) have yellow and russet skins and slightly grainy, solid-textured flesh.

SAFFRON

Intensely aromatic, golden orange spice made from the dried stigmas of a species of crocus. Offers a delicate perfume and golden hue to baked goods. Sold either as threads—the dried stigmas—or in powdered form. Look for products labeled pure saffron.

SHALLOTS

Small member of the onion family with brown skin, white-to-purple flesh and a flavor resembling a cross between sweet onion and garlic.

STOCK, CHICKEN

Flavorful liquid derived from slowly simmering chicken in water, along with herbs and aromatic vegetables. Used as the primary cooking liquid or moistening and flavoring agent in many recipes. Stock may be made fairly easily at home, to be frozen for future use. Many good-quality canned stocks or broths, in regular or concentrated form, are also available; they tend to be saltier than homemade stock, however, so recipes in which they are used should be carefully tasted for seasoning. Excellent stocks may also be found in the freezer section of quality food stores.

SUN-DRIED TOMATOES

When sliced crosswise or halved, then dried in the sun, tomatoes develop an intense, sweet-tart